ALPHABETivities
175 Ready-to-Use Activities
From A to Z

D1298154

Claudia Krause

THE CENTER FOR APPLIED RESEARCH IN EDUCATION, INC.
WEST NYACK, NEW YORK

Library of Congress Cataloging-in-Publication Data

Krause, Claudia.
ALPHABETivities ; 175 ready-to-use activities from
A to Z.

1. English language—Alphabet—Study and teaching.
2. Creative activities and seat work. I. Center for
Applied Research in Education. II. Title.
LB1525.65.K73   1986   372.4'145   85-30912

ISBN 0-87628-149-8

Printed in the United States of America

ABOUT THIS RESOURCE

ALPHABETivities: 175 Ready-to-Use Activities from A to Z gives the pre-K–1 teacher a new and unique way to effectively help children learn the alphabet letters and letter-sound relationships in activities that youngsters find fun and appealing. Designed to fit into *any* reading readiness program, the activities in this remarkable resource are provided in a reproducible format so they are ready-to-go at a moment's notice for instruction of individual students, small groups, or the entire class. In addition to the reproducible page, some activities also require a few simple materials easily found in most classrooms or at home.

These completely preplanned alphabet activities are presented in 26 units, each revolving around a main character and his or her adventures. Between six and nine multisensory activities are provided in each unit, with a broad range of activity types throughout the resource. When children see the letter, feel it (finger tracing), hear it, taste and smell it (cooking), their learning is reinforced in a strong way that emphasizes all learning modes . . . an excellent means to develop each individual child's knowledge of the alphabet in the way he or she learns best.

Reading readiness skills reinforced through the ALPHABETivities include:

auditory letter recognition	knowledge of different vowel sounds	following directions
auditory letter discrimination	writing practice	drawing conclusions
visual letter recognition	sequencing	story recall
upper/lower-case letter recognition	classification	discrimination between real and imaginary events
association of consonant sounds to letters	rhyming	identification of numerals 1–10
	matching	memory
	discrimination of likenesses and differences	
	word recognition	

General skills important to early childhood education also reinforced through the ALPHABETivities include:

shape recognition	creative thinking	finger dexterity
construction	music-making	cutting
coloring	gluing	cooking
creative drawing	painting	folding
printmaking	figure-ground discrimination	bead stringing

After the title of each activity, the Contents lists the one or two major skills developed by the activity. Several other minor skills are being developed by the activity at the same time, however.

Most of the ALPHABETivities can serve as springboards to other curriculum areas to further expand learning. By familiarizing young children with the words for things and places, they will learn about science, math, nutrition and health, history and social studies, geography, and music. The children's own questions and enthusiasm will often lead the way to additional enrichment activities! The following section called "How to Use this Resource" details several enrichment ideas for specific activities.

This book of games and activities for the letters of the alphabet is the result of more than ten years of teaching young children with joy and fun. Children learn the most when they love to do the activities that teach them. I hope you and your class enjoy them!

Claudia Krause

ABOUT THE AUTHOR Claudia Krause, M.A., received her B.A. in Psychology from California State University in Long Beach and her M.A. in Education from the University of Redlands in Redlands, California. She has taught kindergarten through grade 3 for eleven years in the Capistrano Unified School District and also taught Mentally Gifted Children. She developed a psychomotor program for Palisades School and for the Capistrano Unified School District and has been involved in work with the P.T.A. and on faculty committees.

CONTENTS

1

How to Use this Resource

HOW TO USE THIS RESOURCE

ALPHABETivities offers 175 alphabet activities in 26 delightful thematic units, each based on a main character's adventures. Each unit contains between six and nine individual activities designed to be used in sequence for maximum effectiveness because several activities are interrelated within each unit. In this unique resource you will find a wide range of activities from games and puzzles to construction, art and craft activities to cooking experiences.

The first activity in each unit is the easiest one, generally a coloring or cutting and gluing activity. The following activities are more difficult and require increasing recognition and use of the alphabet letter featured.

Each activity is reproducible and appears on one full page (with the exception of nine activities that involve a second page). You make only as many copies of the reproducible page as you need for your group, whether an individual student, a small group, or the entire class. The activity directions are printed in large, primary-size type for easy use by young readers.

Many ALPHABETivities require work directly on the student page (cutting, gluing, manipulating, coloring, drawing). Some of the pages, such as those for some art activities or cooking, are needed for directions only. You can easily expand these activities to integrate them into the whole curriculum (as outlined below), or have the children amplify the illustration through creative drawing or by coloring the illustration. For example, the children might draw a picture of themselves cooking alongside the main character in the cooking page illustration.

Following are some tips for using ALPHABETivities:

Letter-Sound Relationships

To eliminate possible confusion about various letter sounds, the activities use only the hard consonant sounds and the long and short vowel sounds. Consonant digraphs, r-controlled vowels, the schwa sound, and other peculiarities of the English language have been avoided; these can be presented in your own reading program when the children are ready for them.

Both upper-case and lower-case letters are presented in the ALPHA-BETivities to familiarize the children with both. The finger tracing pages also include upper- and lower-case letters.

Vocabulary

The stories for many of the activities employ excellent enrichment vocabulary words. Be sure the children understand the meaning of each new vocabulary word *before* they begin the activity. These vocabulary words are listed below in alphabetical order, by section:

A a
acrobats
Alabama

B b
barbells
brawny
baffled
bookmarks
barley

C c
Connecticut
California
Colorado
collage
casually

D d
delighted
Dalmation
disguise
discarded
derby
desert
disaster
daffy
deviled

E e
enormous
echoing
Eskimo

F f
Fiji
famished

G g
Georgia
ghastly
guacamole
gooseberry
goulash
gruesome
glider
granola
gorp

H h
hilariously

I i
Iguana
igloo

J j
New Jersey
jeep

K k
Kansas
koala
kebabs

L l
Louisiana
lounge
local
lime

M m
Michigan
minister
Montana
munch
morsels
marvelous
muffins

N n
New Mexico
nifty
nickel

O o
otter
octopus
tentacles

P p
pirate
pursues
Pacific

Q q
quilt
quill
quail
quarter
question mark
quiche

R r
reindeer
Rhode Island
Ranger
rascal
raspberries
rash
rooster
radish

S s
sensational
season
South Dakota
spruce
scarlet
scurry
snail

T t
tortoise
Texas
Timberline
Trail
tadpole
tacos

U u
Utah
unicorn
ukulele
unicycle
upside-down
   cake
u-turn

V v
vulture
viewing
valley
vantage
Vermont
vests
violet
variety
visor

W w
West
Wisconsin
sheriff
wanted poster
wandering
witnessed
winding
wagon master
wagon trains
waterfall
waffles
walnuts
woodpecker
wigwam
wick

X x
X-ray
xylophone

Y y
yak
yodeling
Yosemite
yelp
yams

Z z
zebra
Zanzibar
Zurich
zucchini
zinnias
zookeeper
zigzags
ZIP code

Have the children give synonyms for each of the vocabulary words. Also make a point of using the new vocabulary on the day you introduce it and as appropriate thereafter. You will find the children themselves enjoying the use of their new-found words throughout the year!

Illustrations

The illustrations in this resource have been carefully drawn for easy recognition by young children, especially for prereaders. They also provide strong outlines to facilitate coloring and have a humorous flavor to elicit the fun and laughter that adds spice to learning.

Finger Tracing Activities

Finger tracing each letter helps children learn through two learning channels: visual and tactile/kinesthetic. You can also have the children say each letter name softly aloud as they trace to involve hearing/speaking as well.

Collect the tactile alphabet letter sheets in a shoebox for each child. Place the shoeboxes in a convenient location where the children can trace their letters independently each day to reinforce this mode of learning. The complete collection of finger tracing letters will be a very attractive and colorful set of learning tools each child will be proud to work with!

Writing Activities

After each three units of ALPHABETivities a letter practice page helps the children translate finger tracing into printed letters on lines. Traditional Zaner-Bloser letter forms with directional arrows have been provided to maintain consistency between your writing practice program and the activities in this resource.

Art Activities

Each art and craft activity has been designed for use by young children with little or no teacher assistance and has been fully classroom-tested. Most important, each activity culminates in a successful and attractive *child*-made item with all of the charm young children invest in their art. Note that the materials needed are for a single child's project; you need to duplicate amounts for the group size you are working with. Also note that children will need some assistance when cutting out shapes for a few of the activities.

Cooking Activities

As with the art activities, all recipes have been classroom- and kitchen-tested for successful use. Again, it is important to note that the cooking can be entirely performed by the children with little or no teacher assistance. To eliminate possible danger, any cutting with sharp utensils has been designated as a precooking preparation for an adult to perform. In a few cases, children *must* be supervised closely, for example, while cooking at a stove. Wherever necessary, boldface **cautions** have been printed in the activity.

Note that the ingredients needed are for the specific serving size designated; you need to duplicate amounts for the group size you are working with.

As you follow each recipe, explain unfamiliar cooking terms and procedures to the children. For example, explain what it means to "fold" one ingredient into another and why you do this or what a "spatula" is. Discuss why certain ingredients are combined either before or after others.

The recipes have been greatly simplified for easy use by young children and include ingredients that appeal to youngsters. As much as possible, natural and low-sugar/low-salt ingredients have been used. The recipes result in a wide variety of dishes, from snacks to main dishes. As you prepare the dishes, talk about how each contributes to good nutrition and health.

Smell-It Activities

To reinforce each alphabet letter, you can set up a "Smell-It" station in the classroom using items beginning with the alphabet letter, some of which are used in the recipes. Have the children save tasting experiences for the recipe activities or a special "Taste-It" station. By alphabet section, smell-it suggestions are:

A a
apple
B b
banana
bread
blueberries
C c
cinnamon
carob
chocolate
celery
coconut
cheese
corn
D d
dandelion
dill
E e
egg
earth
F f
flowers
fish
G g
grape
garlic
granola
guacamole
gum
gooseberry jelly
goulash

H h
hand lotion
honey
horseradish
ham
cooked
   hamburger
I i
ice cream
ice cube
J j
jellybeans
jam
Jell-O
K k
kraut
ketchup
L l
lemon
lime
licorice
lavender
lollipops
M m
maple syrup
mustard
mayonnaise
marshmallows
N n
nutmeg
nuts (pecan,
   walnut,
    peanut, etc.)

O o
orange
oil
onion
oats
olives
P p
peanut butter
peppermint
pineapple
pepper
Parmesan
   cheese
potato
Q q
quince
R r
rum flavoring
raisins
raspberries
radish
S s
spearmint
strawberry
smoke flavoring
sausage
brown/white
   sugar
salt
T t
tomato
tarragon
tuna

U u
upside-down
   cake
V v
Vaseline
   Petroleum
   Jelly
vanilla
W w
candle wax
watermelon
Worcestershire
   sauce
waffle
walnut
X x
X biscuits
Y y
yams
egg yolk
yogurt
Z z
zucchini
zinnia

Games

Some of the games can be modified for individual play by having the child work against his or her own last score or against a timer.

Take-Home Activities

You can use some of the games as take-home activities for further reinforcement of the skill after use in the classroom. In this way, the child can engage his or her parents and siblings in the learning process and have fun at the same time!

HOW TO INTEGRATE THE ACTIVITIES WITH THE WHOLE CURRICULUM

Most of the activities in this resource can be expanded and integrated with the whole early childhood curriculum for further learning enrichment. While you will no doubt have lots of your own enrichment ideas, the following are specific suggestions for each alphabet section.

A a

GEOGRAPHY:	p. Aa-1—After the activity, first have a child locate your home state on the United States map, then point to the state of Alabama. Discuss how far it is from your home state and its weather and climate.
SCIENCE:	p. Aa-6—Before preparing the recipe, examine an apple. Cut it in half. Name the parts you see. Cut another apple in half crosswise. Compare the apples.
MATH:	p. Aa-6—Before preparing the recipe, talk about the concepts of a whole, halves, quarters and use an apple to demonstrate these.
	p. Aa-6—While preparing the recipe, discuss measurement in teaspoons and cups.
ART:	Make prints of apple halves using tempera paint. Compare and identify the parts of the apple in the prints. Make prints with apple leaves.
MUSIC:	p. Aa-1—After the activity, help the children learn the song "The Daring Young Man on the Flying Trapeze."

B b

LANGUAGE:	After the Bb section, have each child make a B book of construction paper pages cut in the shape of the capital B and stapled together. The child can fill the pages with drawings of B things or glue in B pictures cut from magazines.
SCIENCE:	p. Bb-4—After the activity, compare several butterflies in pictures or in butterfly collections if available.
HEALTH & NUTRITION:	p. Bb-1—After the activity, discuss good nutrition for growing children, and how to make sound food choices. Talk about why the body needs all four Basic Food Groups.
	p. Bb-6—Before preparing the recipe, divide the ingredients into the four Basic Food Groups.

MATH:	p. Bb-2—After the activity, collect several small plastic apples, butterflies, bells, boats, and real nails. Have the children separate these into sets and subsets (for example: nature-made, human-made).
	p. Bb-6—While preparing the recipe, discuss measurement in cups.
ART:	p. Bb-4—After the activity, have the children draw lots of different butterflies using the capital letter B as the wings.
MUSIC:	Sing "Row, Row, Row Your Boat."

C c

GEOGRAPHY:	p. Cc-1—After the activity, first have a child locate your home state on the United States map, then point to the states of Connecticut, California, and Colorado. Discuss the large geographic sections of the U.S. and how these states fit in. Talk about how far it is from your home state to each of these, and the weather and climate of each of these states.
SCIENCE:	p. Cc-1—Study caterpillars (cocoon, chrysalis).
	Study C mammals: cow, cat, canary, crow, crane, cock, camel
HEALTH & NUTRITION:	p. Cc-7—Before preparing the recipe, divide the ingredients into the four Basic Food Groups.
MATH:	p. Cc-3—After the activity, count the hidden objects and add them.
	p. Cc-2- -After the activity, tell how C = 100 in Roman numerals and that $100 is sometimes called a "C note."
	p. Cc-7—While preparing the recipe, discuss measurement in cups, teaspoons, and ounces.
ART:	p. Cc-2—After the activity, encourage the children to make pictures or collages showing as *many* C words as they can think of.

D d

LANGUAGE:	p. Dd-1—After the activity, use a big box of hats, wigs, eyeglasses, moustaches, beards, makeups, and jewelry to create a disguise for each interested child.
	p. Dd-7—Before preparing the recipe, talk about the word "deviled" and what it means in cooking (anything made with hot seasonings; "hot as the devil").
SCIENCE:	p. Dd-1—After the activity, talk about the Dalmation as a breed of dog. Discuss other breeds of dogs and have children tell about their pet dogs.
MATH:	p. Dd-1—After the activity, locate December on a calendar and relate it to the current month and to the rest of the year.
	p. Dd-7—While preparing the recipe, discuss measurement in ounces, tablespoons, and teaspoons.
ART:	After the Dd section, have each child make a Door Book where each page is the door to a special place: the child's room, a castle, teepee, robot's computer, zoo cage, etc. Each door can be cut on three sides to open and a picture of what is inside the door can be glued to the back of the sheet to show through.

E e

HISTORY & SOCIAL STUDIES:

p. Ee-1—After the activity, talk about and visit a chicken farm if possible.

p. Ee-6—After the activity, discuss the Eskimos, where they live, their homes and life style.

SCIENCE:

p. Ee-1—After the activity, discuss various kinds of eggs: chicken, duck, goose, snake, ostrich, dinosaur, Easter, Ukranian Easter, robin, turkey, quail, etc. Make a list of the ones we eat and the ones we do not eat. Open an egg and identify its parts.

MATH:

p. Ee-1—After the activity and the Science enrichment activity, rank the various eggs by size.

Make an addition game using plastic eggs with various numbers of dried beans inside (for example: egg with 3 beans + egg with 4 beans = 7 beans).

p. Ee-3—After the activity, talk about the size relationships among the chicks.

p. Ee-7—While preparing the recipe, talk about measurement in tablespoons.

ART:

Use each cardboard section from an egg carton as the base for a finger puppet of an E creature. Children can make an eagle, elephant, egret, and so forth.

p. Ee-6—After the activity, have the children draw a picture of an Eskimo's igloo, ice floes, and polar bears in an Artic scene. They can use white crayon on dark purple or black paper, or draw on white paper and cover the finished drawing with a light wash of blue or purple poster paint.

MUSIC:

p. Ee-2—After the activity, sing "Old MacDonald" and "The Farmer in the Dell."

F f

GEOGRAPHY:

p. Ff-1—After the activity, first have a child locate the United States on a world map, then point to the island of Fiji. Discuss how far it is from your home and talk about its weather, climate, and people.

SCIENCE:

p. Ff-3—After the activity, study live frogs, flies, and fish. Help children see how legs are attached; number of legs, wings, fins, eyes. Compare these creatures; discuss what each eats and why.

HEALTH & NUTRITION:

After the Ff section, discuss fruits, list them and categorize them. Talk about what fruits do to keep our bodies healthy.

MATH:

pp. Ff-3 & Ff-4—After the activity, write a different number on the back of each fish as its weight. Use these to play an addition game where children add the weights of the fish caught.

p. Ff-6—While preparing the recipe, talk about measurement in ounces and cups.

MUSIC:

Sing "Froggy Went A-Courting."

G g

LANGUAGE: pp. Gg-2 & Gg-3—After the activity, make up silly (not really spooky) ghost stories together.

GEOGRAPHY: p. Gg-1—After the activity, first have a child locate your home state on the United States map, then point to the state of Georgia. Discuss how far it is from your home state, and its weather and climate.

SCIENCE: Study some G animals: goose, goat, gopher, goldfish, groundhog, guinea pig, guppies, gorilla, etc.

HEALTH & NUTRITION: After the Gg section, discuss grains, list them, and categorize them. Talk about what grains do to keep our bodies healthy.

MATH: After the Gg section, have the children look around the classroom and make a list of all the G things they see. Write these on the chalkboard and add them.

Gg-6—While preparing the recipe, talk about measurement in cups.

ART: After the Gg section, paint a very large class mural of a ghostly scene.

MUSIC: p. Gg-5—After the activity, sing "Bill Gordon's Goat."

H h

LANGUAGE: p. Hh-1—After the activity, make up a group story about Happy Harry and some silly misadventures his hair leads him into. Bind the story into a "Harry Book" with illustrations drawn by the children.

SCIENCE: p. Hh-1—Help children list hairy creatures: goat, cave people, guinea pigs, Angora rabbits, yaks, etc. Talk about how hair helps humans and animals (for warmth, protection, beauty). Examine different kinds of hairs under a magnifying glass or microscope.

p. Hh-5—Discuss what various animals eat and why.

ART: After the Hh section, prepare sheets of drawing paper with printed capital and lower-case h's at random and in different directions. Have the children incorporate these h's into individually designed pictures.

I i

LANGUAGE: After the Ii section, read short selections of American Indian poetry. Elicit verbal images of beauty from the children and from them compose a group poem that is Indian-like in tone.

SCIENCE: p. Ii-1—After the activity, study the iguana, where it lives, what it eats, and why.

MATH: Talk about Roman numerals and how I = 1. On the chalkboard write some Roman numerals with I's.

p. Ii-6—While preparing the recipe, discuss measurement in cups and teaspoons.

ART: After the Ii section, show the children pictures of American Indian designs on pottery, rugs, etc. Ask the children to make their own original designs.

J j

GEOGRAPHY: p. Jj-1—After the activity, first have a child locate your home state on the United States map, then point to the state of New Jersey. Discuss how far it is from your home state and its weather and climate.

SCIENCE: p. Jj-2—After the activity, carve a jack o'lantern and examine the pumpkin's contents. Compare the inside of the pumpkin with the contents of another squash gourd. Plant a few pumpkin seeds and watch them grow.

MATH: p. Jj-6—While preparing the recipe, discuss measurement in cups and teaspoons.

MUSIC: Sing "Jingle Bells" (regardless of the season) and have children shake bells while the group sings.

K k

LANGUAGE: p. Kk-2—After the activity, play a guessing game of "What Is in Kelly's Pouch?" Have the leader wear an apron with a large pocket and hold the object in the "pouch" while describing it to the group. The leader then presents the object to the group when it is guessed. The teacher can lead the game until the children are familiar with it.

Play "King for a Day." In this game the "King" commands each person to bring him or her something that begins with the letter K and has other specific characteristics ("something that is very heavy," "something the color of my eyes," etc.).

GEOGRAPHY: p. Kk-1—After the activity, first have a child locate your home state on the United States map, then point to the state of Kansas. Discuss how far it is from your home state and its weather and climate.

SCIENCE: After the Kk section, look at photos of kangaroos, kittens, and koalas in library books and *National Geographic* magazines. Compare the bodies of these animals and discuss the reasons for them. Then have the children pretend to be K animals and provide balls of yarn, leaves, bowls of food, etc. as props.

MATH: p. Kk-3—Count the number of items on the page and add them.

MUSIC: Sing "K-K-K-Katy."

L l

GEOGRAPHY: p. Ll-1—After the activity, first have a child locate your home state on the United States map, then point to the state of Louisiana. Discuss how far it is from your home state and its weather and climate.

SCIENCE: p. Ll-2—After the activity, study lions and ladybugs. How are they the same? different? How might each be helpful to humans?

MATH: Talk about Roman numerals and how L = 50. Write 50, 51, 52, 53, 54, 55 on the board in Roman numerals.

ART: Make leaf prints, lime prints, and pressed leaves collages.

MUSIC: Sing "Here We Go Loopy Loo."

M m

LANGUAGE: p. Mm-2—After the activity, have the children make up new adventures for Matthew and Melinda Mouse that emphasize the letter M (for example, they might use the words movies, Merlin, mousetrap, milk, mozzarella, me).

GEOGRAPHY: pp. Mm-1 & Mm-2—After each activity, first have a child locate your home state on the United States map, then point to the states of Michigan and Montana. Discuss how far it is from your home state to each of these and the weather and climate of these states.

SCIENCE: p. Mm-2—After the activity, bring some live mice to the classroom and have the children observe them.

HEALTH & NUTRITION: p. Mm-2—After the activity, discuss good nutrition for growing children and how to make sound food choices. Talk about how the body needs all four Basic Food Groups.

p. Mm-5—Before preparing the recipe, divide the ingredients into the four Basic Food Groups.

After the Mm-section, explain that M is for meats, which give us protein. What other foods give us protein? (rice and beans, milk, cheese, etc.) How do proteins help our bodies grow?

MATH: Talk about Roman numerals and how M = 1000. Write the year on the board in Roman numerals.

p. Mm-1—After the activity, locate May on a calendar and relate it to the current month and to the rest of the year.

MUSIC: p. Mm-5—After preparing the recipe, sing the Campbell's Soup jingle with the words "M-m-m good! M-m-m good! That's what Melinda's muffins are: M-m-m good!"

N n

LANGUAGE: After the Nn section and the SCIENCE activity below, have the children illustrate individual Nest Books showing parent animals and their babies. Then have the children pretend to be mothers/fathers and babies in a nest. Make some big soft nests of pillows and blankets.

GEOGRAPHY: p. Nn-1—After the activity, first have a child locate your home state on the United States map, then point to the state of New Mexico. Discuss how far it is from your home state and its weather and climate.

SCIENCE: After the Nn section, study a variety of bird nests. Then talk about nests of other animals: squirrels, rats, rabbits, chimpanzees, etc.

MATH: p. Nn-7—While preparing the recipe, discuss measurement in quarts (gallons, pints), cups, and ounces.

O o

SCIENCE: p. Oo-3—After the activity, study the octopus, otter, and ostrich. How are they the same? different? How might each help humans?

MATH: p. Oo-6—While preparing the recipe, talk about measurement in cups, teaspoons, and tablespoons.

ART: After the Oo section, give the class a big bowl of flat O macaroni shapes. Have the children glue them in individual designs or pictures on sheets of construction paper. Let dry, then paint with poster paint and sprinkle with glitter.

P p

**HISTORY &
SOCIAL
STUDIES:**

p. Pp-1—After the activity, talk about pirates, when they lived, where they came from, and how they lived.

p. Pp-3—After the activity, use the eye patches and head scarves to play pirate.

GEOGRAPHY:

p. Pp-1—After the activity, first have a child locate the United States on a world map, then point to the Pacific Ocean. Discuss how far it is from your home state to the Pacific Ocean and some of the large countries that border the Pacific.

MATH:

p. Pp-5—While preparing the recipe, discuss measurement in cups.

ART:

p. Pp-1—After the activity, have each child make an original picture of the Pacific Ocean and P words for things you might find there (for example: puffer fish, penguin, pearl diver, palm trees, pieces of driftwood, pebbles, palm-thatched huts, etc.). Children can do individual crayon resist drawings (with a wash of poster paint), or the whole class can work on a Pacific Ocean wall mural.

P is for printmaking. Children can make thumbprint pictures, monoprints, fruit and vegetable prints, etc.

P is for paper. Children can make handmade paper.

Q q

SCIENCE:

p. Qq-4—After the activity, study the quail, its egg, feathers, and habits. Call your local wildlife organization to find out where quail may be observed in your area, then take a field trip.

MATH:

After the Qq section, make 1 to 10 follow-the-dot crown drawings on paper.

p. Qq-3—After the activity, count the hidden objects and add them.

p. Qq-6—While preparing the recipe, discuss measurement in pounds.

ART:

After the Qq section, make crowns with paper and glue-on sequins, glitter, gold foil, stars, etc., and use these crowns for dramatic play.

R r

LANGUAGE:

After the Rr section, have the class make up a story of a barking dog—"R-r-r-r." As often as possible, the children can bark in unison. (For example: "Roger is a big dog. When he barks, the neighbors all hear him. 'R-r-r-r.' One day he went into the forest near his home. He heard a strange noise, so he said, 'R-r-r-r.'". . . .)

GEOGRAPHY:

p. Rr-1—After the activity, first have a child locate your home state on the United States map, then point to the state of Rhode Island. Discuss how far it is from your home state and its weather and climate.

SCIENCE:

After the Rr section, study reindeer, which are fascinating mammals. Obtain some reindeer books from the library and study the reindeer's body and habits. What are the purposes of its horns? (protection, intimidation, camouflage, to shake a tree to get food, etc.) Compare horned animals—the reindeer, elk, moose, antelope, mountain goats, sheep. How are their horns the same? different?

p. Rr-5—Bring a live rabbit to school for the children to observe and cuddle.

MATH:	p. Rr-3—Identify the geometric shapes used. Then ask the children to name items in the classroom with each of these shapes.
	p. Rr-6—While preparing the recipe, discuss measurement in cups, tablespoons, and teaspoons.

S s

LANGUAGE:	p. Ss-4—After the activity, make Sun Books where each page is devoted to a "sun" word with an illustration (for example: sunglasses, Sunday school, sunbathing, suntan lotion, sunflower, sunsuit, etc.).
GEOGRAPHY:	p. Ss-1—After the activity, first have a child locate your home state on a United States map, then point to the state of South Dakota. Discuss how far it is from your home state and its weather and climate.
SCIENCE:	p. Ss-1—After the activity, study snowflakes and examine some under a microscope if possible.
	p. Ss-2—After the activity, study different types of animal homes and the reasons for them (for example: protection, animal size, availability of food, etc.). Investigate the materials animals use to build their homes and how they use them.
	After the Ss section, study whatever S creatures the children are interested in. Suggestions: snakes, sowbugs (prehistoric creatures that still exist), spiders, swallows, sunfish, starfish, snails, swordfish, sand dollars, sea urchins, sea cucumbers, spiney oysters, salamanders.
MATH:	p. Ss-1—After the activity, cut snowflakes from folded paper and talk about the geometric shapes used.
ART:	After the Ss section, make big sunflower paintings.
MUSIC:	Sing "Sipping Cider Through a Straw."

T t

GEOGRAPHY:	p. Tt-1—After the activity, first have a child locate your home state on a United States map, then point to the state of Texas. Discuss how far it is from your home state and its weather and climate.
SCIENCE:	Study T things in nature: various trees, the tortoise, turtledove, tornado, tuna.
HEALTH:	p. Tt-3—After the activity, study teeth—their variety (compare teeth among the children and adults in the class; compare animal teeth), dental care, how teeth work, etc.
MATH:	p. Tt-5—While preparing the recipe, discuss measurement in pounds and cups.
ART:	After the Tt section, make handmade toys from scraps and cloth.

U u

LANGUAGE:	p. Uu-1—After the activity, study the prefix uni-. "Uni- means one, so a unicorn has *1 horn,* a unicycle has *1 wheel,* a uniform means that all the suits have *1 form.*"
	pp. Uu-1, Uu-2, Uu-3—After any of these activities, have the children make up original unicorn stories using as many U words as possible.
GEOGRAPHY:	p. Uu-1—After the activity, first have a child locate your home state on a United States map, then point to the state of Utah. Discuss how far it is from your home state and its weather and climate.

MATH:	p. Uu-5—While preparing the recipe, discuss measurement in cups.
MUSIC:	p. Uu-2—After the activity, accompany the children's favorite records or songs with their ukuleles

V v

LANGUAGE:	p. Vv-5—After the activity, explain the wartime use of the expression "V for Victory" and the hand signal that goes with it.
GEOGRAPHY:	p. Vv-1—After the activity, first have a child locate your home state on a United States map, then point to the state of Vermont. Discuss how far it is from your home state and its weather and climate.
SCIENCE:	After the Vv section, study these: vulture, vampire (bats), volcano. These are all emotion-packed subjects and the children will enjoy them.
MATH:	Talk about Roman numerals and how V = 5. On the chalkboard write some numbers incorporating V for 5.
	p. Vv-7—While preparing the recipe, discuss measurement in tablespoons and cups.
ART:	After the Vv section, have the children make pictures using as many Vs as possible in different positions. Then count the number of Vs in each picture.
	p. Vv-4—After the activity, make valentines (at any time of year).

W w

LANGUAGE:	After the Ww section, recite the nursery rhyme "Wee Willie Winkie" with the class.
HISTORY & SOCIAL STUDIES:	p. Ww-2—After the activity, talk about the Pennsylvania Dutch hex signs posted on houses and barns to ward off evil.
	p. Ww-4—After the activity, talk about what life in the early West was like, how home life differed from present home life, what children did for fun, how outlaws lived, the journey of the wagon trains, etc.
GEOGRAPHY:	p. Ww-1—After the activity, first have a child locate your home state on a United States map, then point out the state of Wisconsin and the West. Discuss how far it is from your home state to Wisconsin and the West, and the weather and climate of these two areas. Discuss which states comprise the West.
SCIENCE:	After the Ww section, study W creatures: wildebeest, wasp, wart hog, whale.
	p. Ww-2—After the activity, talk about different kinds of wheels and their uses: cartwheels, Ferris wheels, car wheels, bike wheels, wagon wheels, wheel clock parts, etc.
MATH:	p. Ww-8—While preparing the recipe, discuss measurement in cups and teaspoons.
ART:	After the Ww section, have the children make a variety of Ws with several different objects (for example: fork, comb, chopstick, sponge, rubber eraser) on fingerpaint-covered fingerpaint paper.

X x

LANGUAGE: After the Xx section, talk about how X stands for "kiss." Make a story of X = kiss stories or pictures, and be sure to include lots of OOO (for hugs)!

SCIENCE: p. Xx-1—After the activity, elicit children's ideas of what creatures from outer space might look and be like and why.

p. Xx-1—After the activity, look at photos in *National Geographic* of United States space exploration. Look at a map of our solar system and locate the Earth and each of the planets you study.

MATH: Talk about Roman numerals and how X = 10. On the chalkboard write some Roman numerals with Xs.

p. Xx-5—While preparing the recipe, discuss measurement in cups, teaspoons, and tablespoons.

ART: After the Xx section, have the children do cross-stitch on fabric or large needlepoint canvas using yarn and a blunt needlepoint needle. They can make simple designs or a picture made up of Xs.

Y y

GEOGRAPHY: p. Yy-1—After the activity, first have a child locate your home state on a United States map, then point to Yosemite National Park in California. Discuss how far it is from your home state and the weather, climate, and special features of the park (high-walled valley, waterfall, wildlife).

SCIENCE: p. Yy-1—After the activity, study the yak.

MATH: p. Yy-4—Count the items and add them.

p. Yy-6—While preparing the recipe, discuss measurement in teaspoons.

ART: After the Yy section, give the children various Ys cut from different-colored construction paper and have them glue them to a sheet of paper in different designs or compile a collage.

MUSIC: p. Yy-1—After the activity, listen to records of yodeling, then have the children try to yodel!

Z z

GEOGRAPHY: p. Zz-1—After the activity, first have a child locate the United States on a world map, then point to the island of Zanzibar (off the east coast of Africa) and the city of Zurich in Switzerland. Discuss how far it is from your home state to each of these, and the weather and climate of each place. Talk about the continents and point out each one.

SCIENCE: After the Zz section, study zigzag lightning (Why does it zigzag?) and the zipper (examine it and take one apart to see how it works).
p. Zz-4—After the activity, talk about the things animals do when they play.

MATH:	p. Zz-5—After the activity, elicit the meaning of zero from the children and demonstrate it in as many ways as you can (for example: emptiness, nothingness, blank).
ART:	p. Zz-1—After the activity, have the children make individual Zoo Books in which each page is devoted to an animal. The books can have pages stapled into a binding or a long sheet of paper can be accordion folded to make pages. Some children may wish to have a 26-page book with an animal for each letter of the alphabet on consecutive pages.
MUSIC:	Sing "Zippety Do Dah."
ART:	After you have completed all A–Z activities, provide lots of alphabet macaroni for the children to use in *any* way they like. Provide white glue, little pieces of wood, cloth, paper, crayons, paints, etc., and let the children be inventive. One idea: Have the children make very simple follow-the-dot puzzles. Colored alphabet macaroni can be made by following the directions on page Nn-5.

2

Activity Pages
A–Z

Finger Tracing the Letters A a

Reproduce this page for each child in your class. Have each child cut along the dotted line and discard the teacher directions. Then help each child one glue apple seeds on the heavy black lines using white glue and making sure not to cover up the direction arrows.

When the glue is dry, have each child trace over the letters using the first finger and following the directions indicated by the numbered arrows.

Place the finished letter sheet with the child's name on the back in a shoebox for each child and locate the boxes in a convenient place where the children can practice tracing the letters daily. This will help them remember the names of the letters and the correct way to form them.

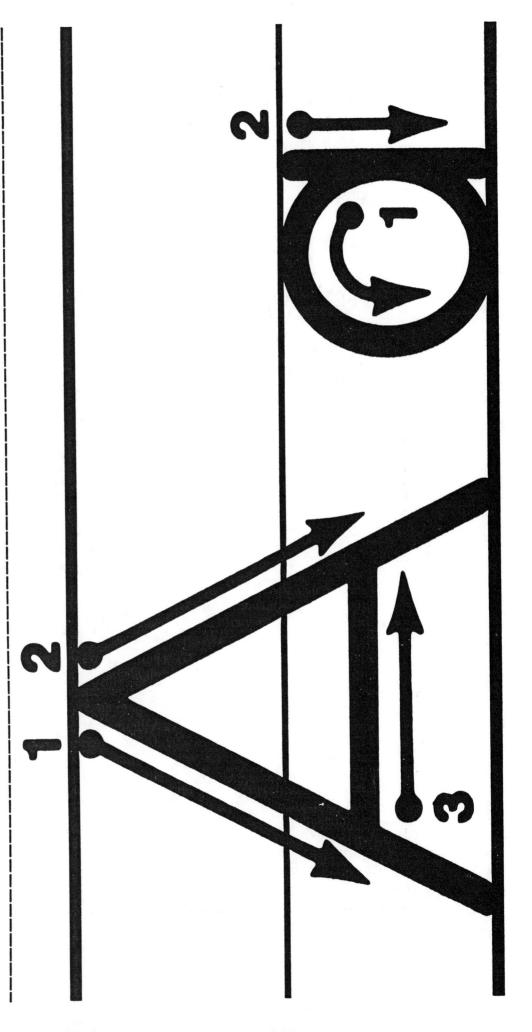

Name _____

April and Andy the Acrobats

April and Andy are acrobats in the Alabama circus. They have a great act. Andy throws April into the air and catches her with his arms. Color Andy's and April's costumes for them.

Name _____

Apple Art

April and Andy love to eat apples between their acts. Here's a yummy apple for you to make. Here's what you do:

1. Using white glue, begin gluing a string of red yarn at the dot in the center of the apple. Continue gluing the yarn in a tight circle until the whole apple is covered.
2. Glue a piece of brown yarn on the stem.
3. Glue short strips of green yarn side by side on the leaves.
4. Place a thick book on top of a sheet of waxed paper on top of the apple. Let the glue dry completely, then remove the book.

Name _____

Alexander and Amy Match Balloons

Alexander and Amy like to collect circus balloons. Which ones do you think they will choose? Cut out all of the balloons and glue them on the strings. Make sure all of Alexander's balloons and all of Amy's balloons are alike in some way.

Name _____

The Apple Game (For 2 players)

To play the apple game, here's what you do:

1. Place a marker for each player on the capital **A**.
2. The first player tosses a penny in the air. If it lands face up, he or she moves ahead 2 spaces. If it lands face down, he moves ahead 1 space. The player must name the **A** picture in the space he lands on.
3. The second player takes a turn in the same way. The first player to land on the lower-case **a** in the center is the winner.

Name _____

A a Puzzle

To solve this puzzle, color the capital A spaces red and color the lower-case **a** spaces green. What **A** picture did you find?

Name _____

April and Andy's Applesauce (Serves 8)

You need:

12 apples (peeled and sliced)
 2 teaspoons cinnamon
 ¼ cup water
 ¼ cup honey (*optional*)

Directions:
Place the apples, cinnamon, and water in a saucepan. Simmer over low heat until tender (about 20 minutes). Stir several times during the cooking. Mash the apples into applesauce with a table fork and add honey as you mash if you like.

Finger Tracing the Letters B b

Reproduce this page for each child in your class. Have each child cut along the dotted line and discard the teacher directions. Then help each one glue dried beans on the heavy black lines using white glue and making sure not to cover up the direction arrows.

When the glue is dry, have each child trace over the letters using the first finger and following the directions indicated by the numbered arrows.

Place the finished letter sheet with the child's name on the back in a shoebox for each child and locate the boxes in a convenient place where the children can practice tracing the letters daily. This will help them remember the names of the letters and the correct way to form them.

Name _____

Barry Beaglehopper

Barry Beaglehopper was a bag of bones until he started working out with his barbells. Now he's brawny and beautiful. Color Barry's barbells a color that begins with the sound of **b.**

Name _____

Barry Beaglehopper's Barbells

Barry likes to work out with his barbells, but he'll only lift barbells that have pictures with the sound of **b** on them. Help Barry find the **b** weights. When you find them, color them, cut them out, and help Barry practice lifting them by placing the barbells in Barry's hands on page Bb-1.

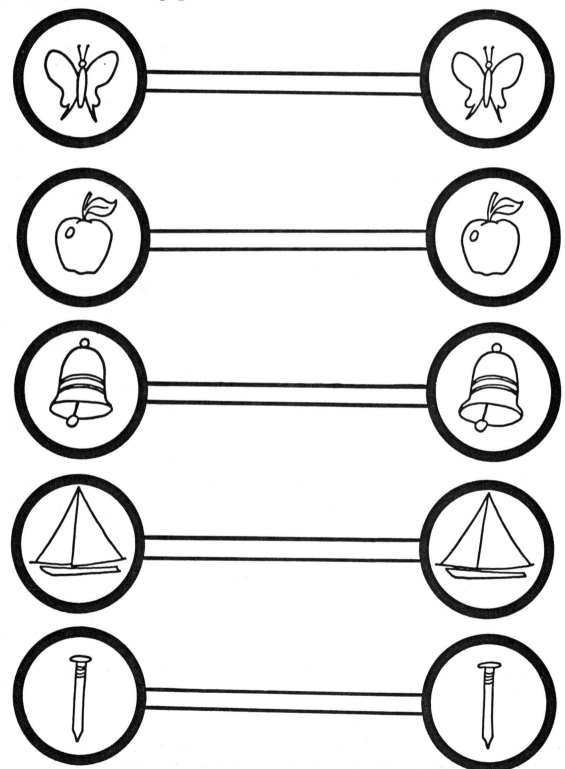

Name _____

Help Barry Match Letters

Barry is a little baffled by all of the letters on this page. He wants to find the letters in each row that are exactly the same. Help Barry by looking at the first letter in each row and circling the matching letters in that row. (There is more than one match in each row.)

B	P B D O B R
F	R E I F L F
b	a h b c d
f	h d f k r f
M	N E M K M F
D	D O D R B C
m	n e r m m u
d	h d c b o d

Name _____

Barry Beaglehopper's Bookmarks

Barry Beaglehopper likes to read as well as lift barbells. Here are some of Barry's bookmarks for you to make. Decorate them with pictures of things that begin with the **b** sound. One bookmark has been started for you. Be sure to use some colors that start with the **b** sound.

Name _____

B b Puzzle

To solve this puzzle, color all of the capital **B** spaces blue. What **b** picture did you find?

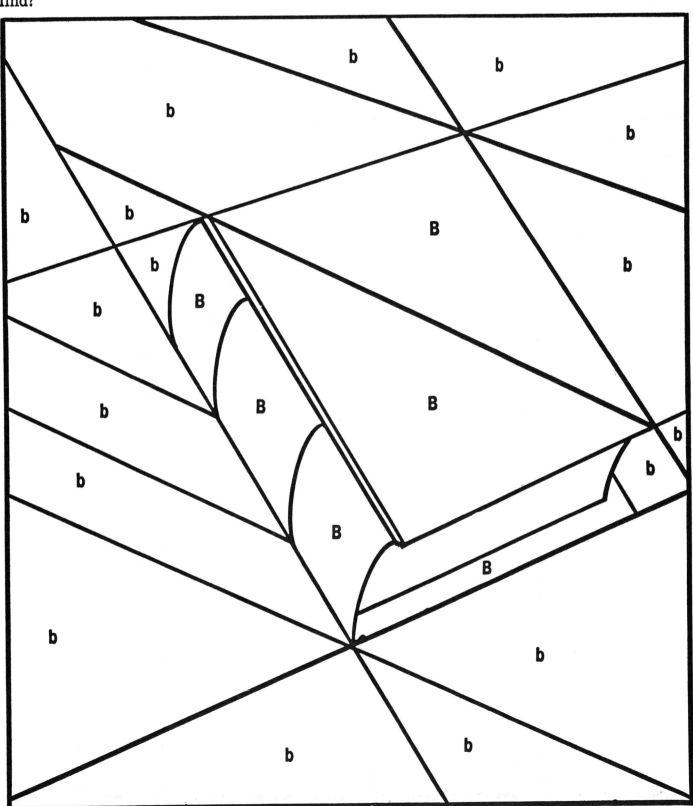

Name _____

Barry Beaglehopper's Buttered Barley
(Serves 8)

You need:

½ cup butter
1 onion (chopped)
1 16-ounce package pearl barley
4 cups water

Directions:
Melt the butter in a skillet and brown the onion and barley. Place this mixture into a 3- to 4-quart baking dish and add the water. Bake at 350° for 1 hour.

Finger Tracing the Letters C c

Reproduce this page for each child in your class. Have each child cut along the dotted line and discard the teacher directions. Then help each one glue colored hard candies or dried corn on the heavy black lines using white glue and making sure not to cover up the direction arrows.

When the glue is dry, have each child trace over the letters using the first finger and following the directions indicated by the numbered arrows.

Place the finished letter sheet with the child's name on the back in a shoebox for each child and locate the boxes in a convenient place where the children can practice tracing the letters daily. This will help them remember the names of the letters and the correct way to form them.

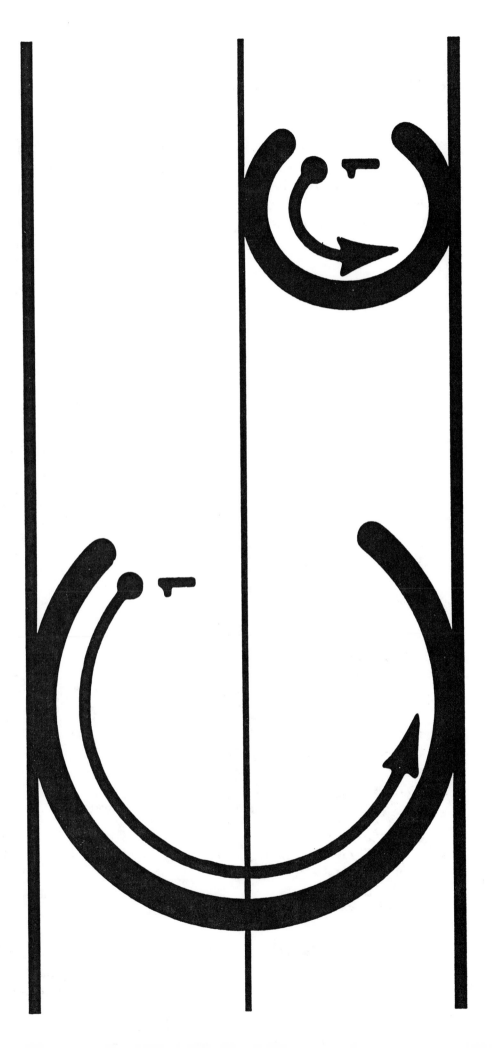

Name _____

Carrie Caterpillar

Carrie Caterpillar has been slowly crawling from Connecticut to California. She has already traveled through Colorado. She would like to have some colorful new clothes before she arrives. Help Carrie by coloring her clothes on this page.

Name _____

Carrie Caterpillar's C Collage

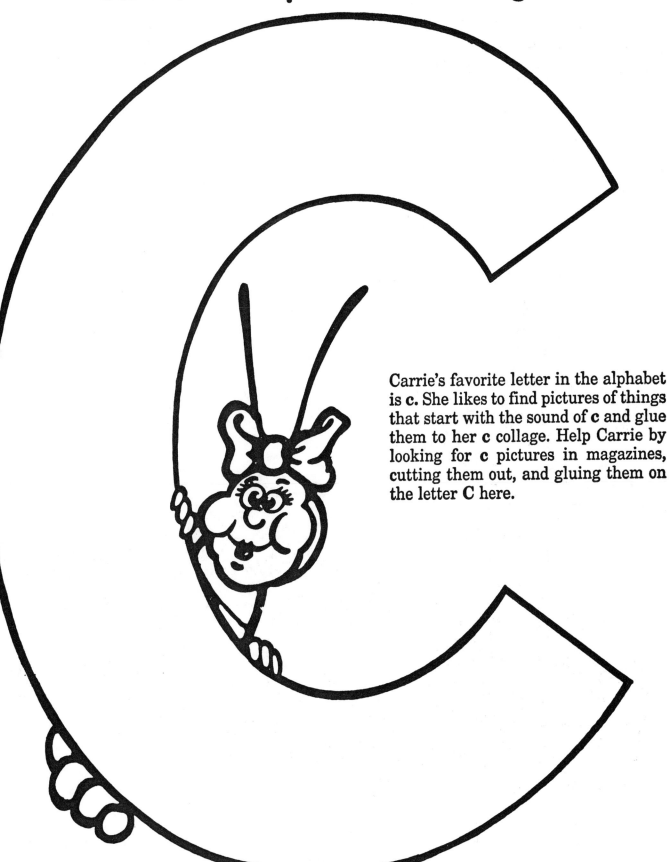

Carrie's favorite letter in the alphabet is **c**. She likes to find pictures of things that start with the sound of **c** and glue them to her **c** collage. Help Carrie by looking for **c** pictures in magazines, cutting them out, and gluing them on the letter **C** here.

Name _____

Help Carrie Find Hidden Objects

Carrie Caterpillar crawls in some very interesting places. One day she found herself along the edge of this creek. The grass was quite high on both sides, and she thought she saw some objects hidden in the grass. Help Carrie find all 7 hidden objects in this picture. Color each one using one color. Then finish coloring the page with other colors if you like.

ANSWERS: ladybug, matchstick, book, mushroom, flower, fork, mitten.

Name _____

Carrie's Candle Craft

Carrie travels quite casually on her trips, but she always takes a candle with her for light. You can make a model of Carrie's candle. Here's what you do:

1. Glue an empty toilet paper tube to the bottom of a paper plate using white glue.
2. Glue a paper circle the same size as the top of the tube to the top. Let this dry for several hours.
3. Place ½ cup of warm water into a large bowl and add 2 cups of Ivory Snow. Let this mixture stand for 2 minutes.
4. With a hand beater, whip the soap until frothy. Gradually add ½ cup more warm water until the soap stands in peaks.
5. Scoop the soap mixture with your hand and completely cover the toilet paper tube with it.
6. Sprinkle glitter all over the wet candle model.
7. Cut out a red construction paper or cellophane flame and insert it in the top of the candle. Let this dry overnight.

Name _____

Carrie's C Game (For 2 players)

You can play this thinking game with a friend. Here's what you do:

1. Glue the card sheet below onto a piece of heavy paper and let dry.
2. Cut out the cards, shuffle them, and spread them on a table face down.
3. The first player turns 2 cards face up to try to make a pair. If the cards match, he keeps them and the second player takes a turn. If they do not match, he turns them face down and the second player looks for a pair. The player with the most pairs of **c** cards wins.

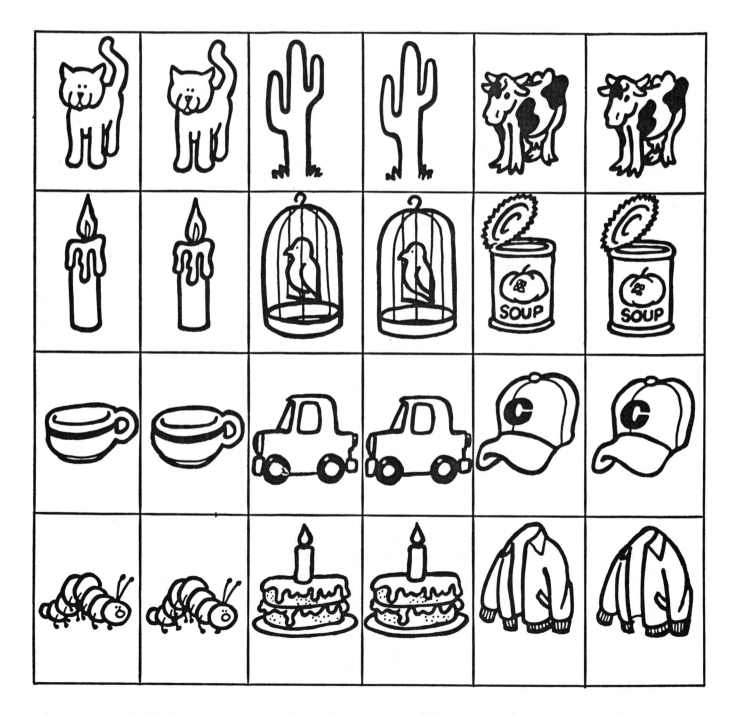

Name _____

C c Puzzle

To solve this puzzle, color the lower-case **c** spaces yellow and color the *empty* spaces any color you would like. What **c** picture did you find?

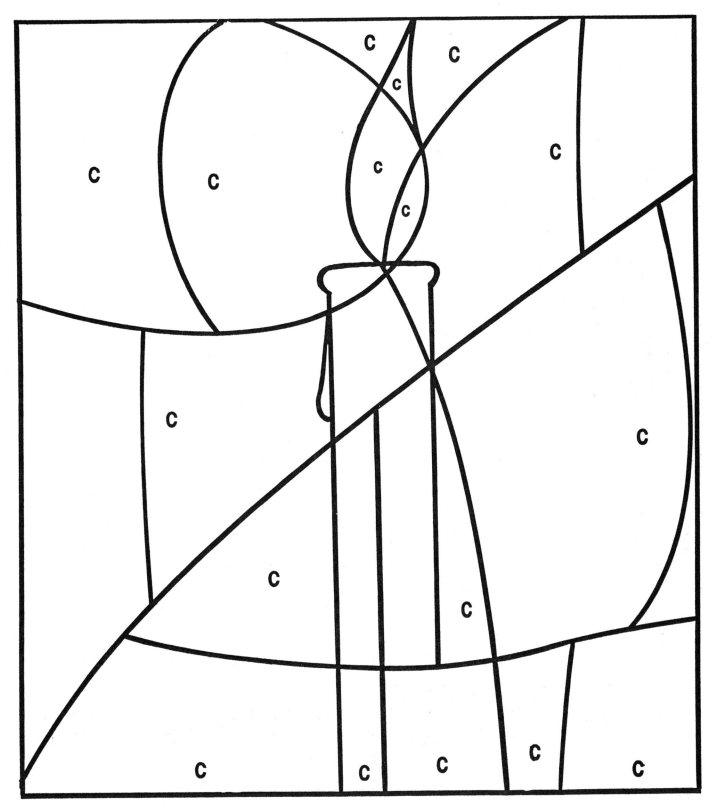

Name _____

Carrie's Carrot Cake
(Serves 10–12)

You need:

2 cups sugar
1½ cups vegetable oil
4 eggs
2 cups flour
2 teaspoons baking soda
2 teaspoons baking powder
2 teaspoons cinnamon
1 teaspoon salt
3 cups grated carrots
½ cup chopped walnuts

For frosting you need:

¼ stick butter
5 ounces cream cheese
½ 16-ounce box powdered sugar
½ teaspoon vanilla
8-ounce can crushed pineapple

Directions:
Mix the sugar and oil in a large bowl with **a hand beater or electric mixer (use caution).** Add the eggs, one at a time, and beat well. Add the dry ingredients and mix well. Add the carrots and chopped nuts. Mix until all of the ingredients are well blended. Pour the mixture into a loaf cake pan and bake in a 325° oven for 45 minutes. Let the cake cool for an hour, then frost.

Directions:
Place the butter, cream cheese, powdered sugar, and vanilla in a medium-sized bowl and mix with an electric mixer **(use caution)** until well blended. Add all but **3** tablespoons crushed pineapple to this mixture and blend with the mixer. Frost the cooled carrot cake with a table knife or spatula. Use the rest of the crushed pineapple to make a **C** on top of the cake.

Name _____

A B C Letter Review

Practice writing these letters on the lines below. You have mastered the letters A, a, B, b, C, c. Congratulations!

A A A

a a a

B B B

b b b

C C C

C C C

Finger Tracing the Letters D d

Reproduce this page for each child in your class. Have each child cut along the dotted line and discard the teacher directions. Then help each one glue different-colored paper puncher dots on the heavy black lines using white glue and making sure not to cover up the direction arrows.

When the glue is dry, have each child trace over the letters using the first finger and following the directions indicated by the numbered arrows.

Place the finished letter sheet with the child's name on the back in a shoebox for each child and locate the boxes in a convenient place where the children can practice tracing the letters daily. This will help them remember the names of the letters and the correct way to form them.

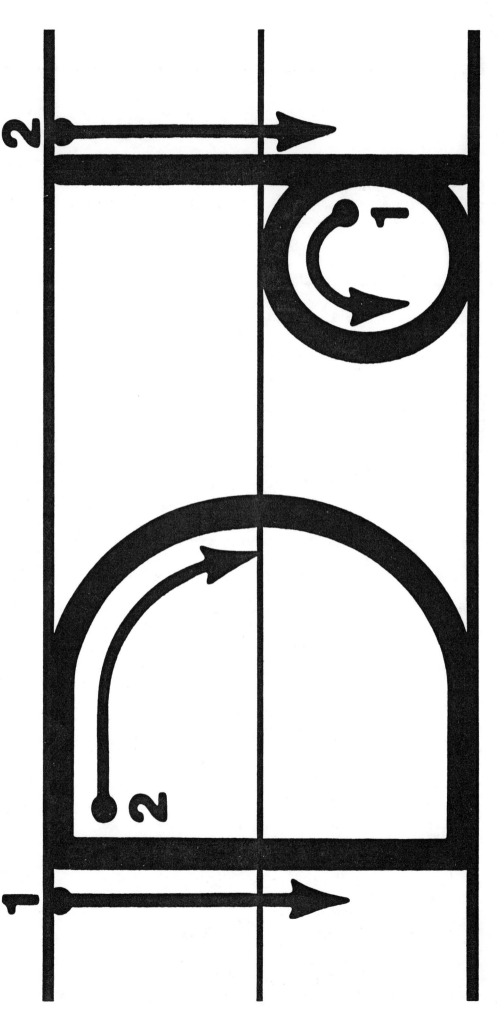

Name _____

Detective Dan and Daisy

Detective Dan is delighted to have a Dalmation dog for his partner. However, Detective Dan wants to give his Dalmation dog, Daisy, a disguise. He found a discarded derby in the desert last December. Write a lower-case **d** on the dog's derby, then color the whole picture.

Name _____

Daisy's Maze Puzzle

Detective Dan's partner Daisy was given the delightful duty of finding a missing shipment of dog bones! Help Daisy by finding the right path to the missing bones. Start at the picture of Daisy and find the correct path. Remember: you cannot cross over any lines. Good luck!

Name _____

Match Daisy's Derbies

Daisy has a dreadful problem! She leaves her derby hats all over the den. She soon realized the den was a disaster and decided to do something about it. To help Daisy, color and cut out all of the derby hats and the hatracks. Then glue the hats on the hatracks so that all of the hats on each rack are alike.

Name _____

Daisy's Bones

Daisy was rewarded for finding the missing shipment of dog bones. Guess what she received? You guessed it — some of those tasty bones! She has dug three holes in the backyard and she needs to decide where the bones should be hidden. Cut out the bones at the bottom of this page and glue them in the holes so that the bones in each hole are alike in some way.

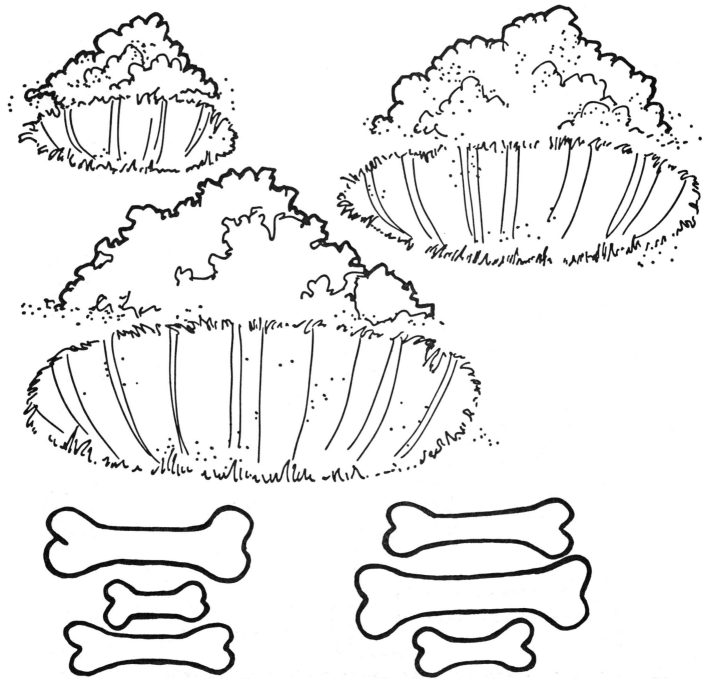

Name _____

Detective Dan's Dreams

Detective Dan has daffy dreams! He only dreams about things starting with the **d** sound. Find the pictures with the **d** sound, cut them out, and glue them inside the dream cloud. Then draw your *own* **d** picture in the dream!

Name _____

D d Puzzle

To solve this puzzle, color the capital **D** spaces gray and color the lower-case **d** spaces blue. What **d** picture did you find?

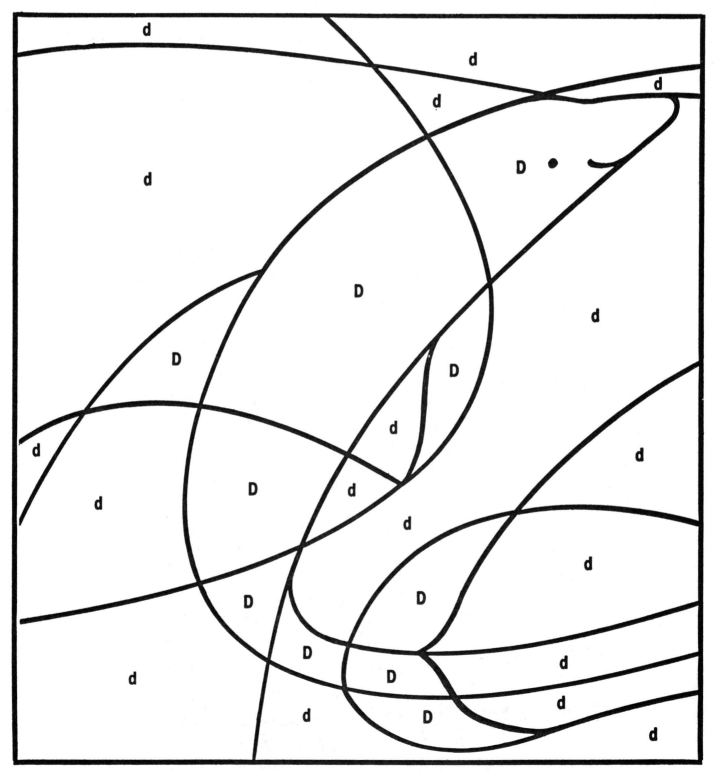

Name _____

Detective Dan's Deviled Ham Dip
(Serves 4–6)

You need:

1 3-ounce package cream cheese
1 4½-ounce can deviled ham
1 tablespoon ketchup
1 teaspoon Worcestershire sauce

Directions:

Mix all of the ingredients with a table fork in a bowl. Make sure to mix it until it is smooth. Then dip sliced fresh vegetables or crackers into the dip!

Finger Tracing the Letters E e

Reproduce this page for each child in your class. Have each child cut along the dotted line and discard the teacher directions. Then help each one glue dried eggshell pieces on the heavy black lines using white glue and making sure not to cover up the direction arrows.

When the glue is dry, have each child trace over the letters using the first finger and following the directions indicated by the numbered arrows.

Place the finished letter sheet with the child's name on the back in a shoebox for each child and locate the boxes in a convenient place where the children can practice tracing the letters daily. This will help them remember the names of the letters and the correct way to form them.

Name _____

Elaine's Enormous Egg

Farmer Edward went into his barn one morning and discovered that his favorite hen, Elaine, had laid an enormous egg. He could hardly believe his eyes! Suddenly the egg cracked! Find out what was inside by first making an egg like Elaine's. Cut out the egg on the black line, then separate the egg into 2 pieces by cutting on the crack line. Now connect the pieces by putting a paper brad through the dot and then through the letter E. Now turn to page Ee-2 and help Elaine find her baby chick.

Name _____

Find Elaine's Baby Chick

Cracking sounds were echoing all over the barn, and baby chicks were everywhere! Elaine was eager to find her baby, but she could only recognize it by the **E** on its down. Find Elaine's chick for her, cut it out, and glue it on the shell you made in activity **Ee-1**. Make sure the chick's head and its **E** show out of the shell.

Name _____

Farmer Edward's Chicken Pens

Farmer Edward wanted to build special pens for all of his chicks. He built a large pen, a medium-sized pen, and a small pen. Help Farmer Edward place these chicks in the pens. Cut out and glue 2 chicks of the same size in a pen that fits them best.

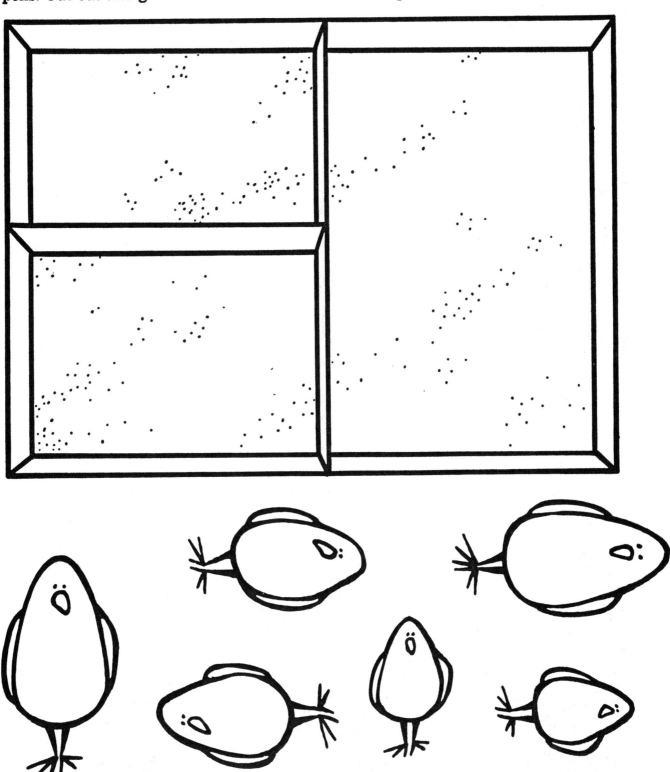

Name _____

Elaine's Egg Game (For 2 players)

To play Elaine's egg game, follow these directions:

1. Cut out the egg below and glue it to a piece of heavy paper or cardboard.
2. Place the egg gameboard on a smooth floor.
3. The first player stands directly over the gameboard and drops a penny from waist height. If the penny lands in a space, the player names the **e** picture and gets the point in the circle in that space if he or she is correct. Then the second player takes a turn.
4. If the penny lands on a line or off the gameboard, the player takes turns until it lands in an **e** space. The first player to earn 10 points wins!

Name _____

Egg Art

Here's what you do to make egg art:

1. Blow up an oval balloon.
2. Tie a long string to the end of the balloon and tie the other end to something strong (like a light fixture) so the balloon can hang down. Place newspapers on the floor under the hanging balloon.
3. In a small bowl, stir ¼ cup white glue and ¼ cup warm water together with a spoon.
4. Dip colored string, embroidery floss, or thin colored yarn into the glue mixture.
5. Wrap the string all over and around the balloon until it covers the balloon as shown in this picture. Let this dry for several hours until the string is hard.
6. Pop the balloon with a needle, gently peel off the balloon, and tie the egg shape at the top with a piece of clear plastic fishing line. Daub clear nail polish on the knot so it won't untie. Hang your egg art in your favorite spot!

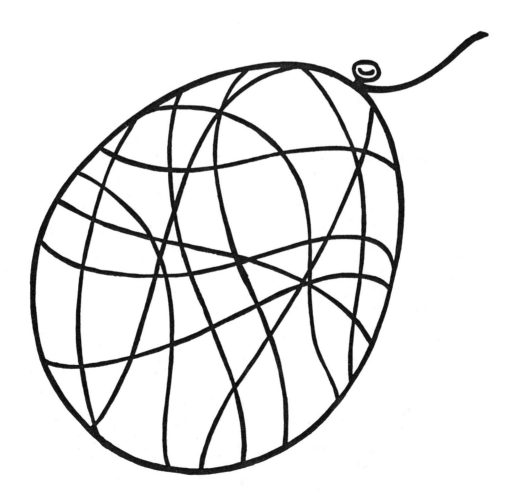

Name _____

E e Puzzle

To solve this puzzle, color the capital **E** spaces brown. Color the lower-case **e** spaces light blue. What **e** picture did you find?

Name _____

Elaine's Egg in a Nest
(Serves 1)

You need:

1 piece of bread
2 tablespoons butter
1 egg

Directions:
With a table knife, cut a large hole in the center of a piece of bread and butter one side. Melt 1 tablespoon butter in a nonstick frying pan. Place the bread with the buttered side up in the pan. Crack the egg into the "nest" (hole) and fry. Use a flipper to turn the egg in a nest over and then cook it on the other side.

Finger Tracing the Letters F f

   Reproduce this page for each child in your class. Have each child cut along the dotted line and discard the teacher directions. Then help each one glue dried flowers or feathers on the heavy black lines using white glue and making sure not to cover up the direction arrows.

   When the glue is dry, have each child trace over the letters using the first finger and following the directions indicated by the numbered arrows.

   Place the finished letter sheet with the child's name on the back in a shoebox for each child and locate the boxes in a convenient place where the children can practice tracing the letters daily. This will help them remember the names of the letters and the correct way to form them.

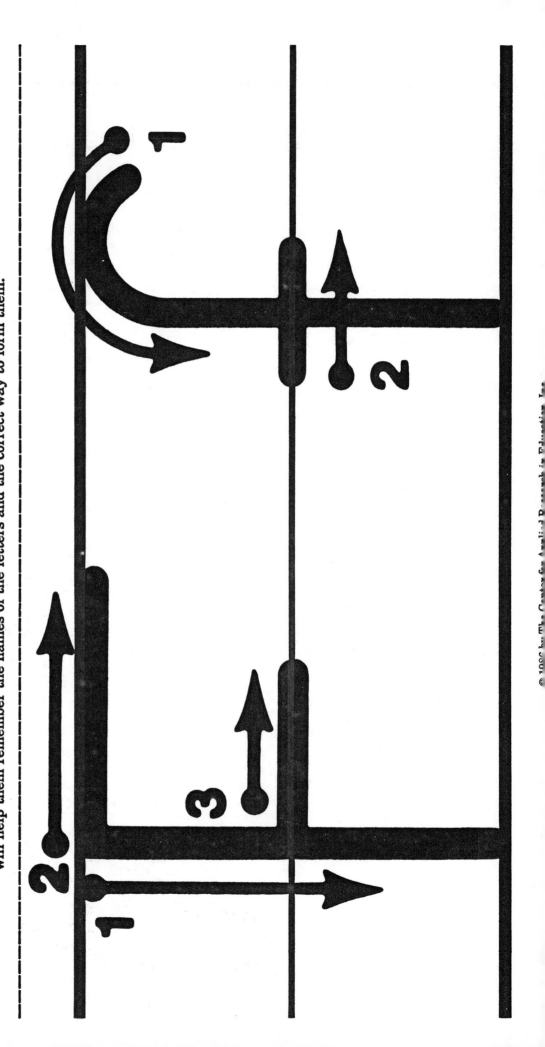

Name _____

Fanny Frog Puppet

Fanny Frog is fascinated by flies. She would travel as far as Fiji to fetch a few! Help put Fanny together so she can search for flies. Here's what you do:

1. Color Fanny green, then cut around her head and body on this page.
2. Glue her head to the bottom flap of a paper bag. Make sure the part that folds over is under her chin.
3. Glue Fanny's body onto the front of the paper bag just under the flap.
4. Fanny Frog is ready to fetch flies!

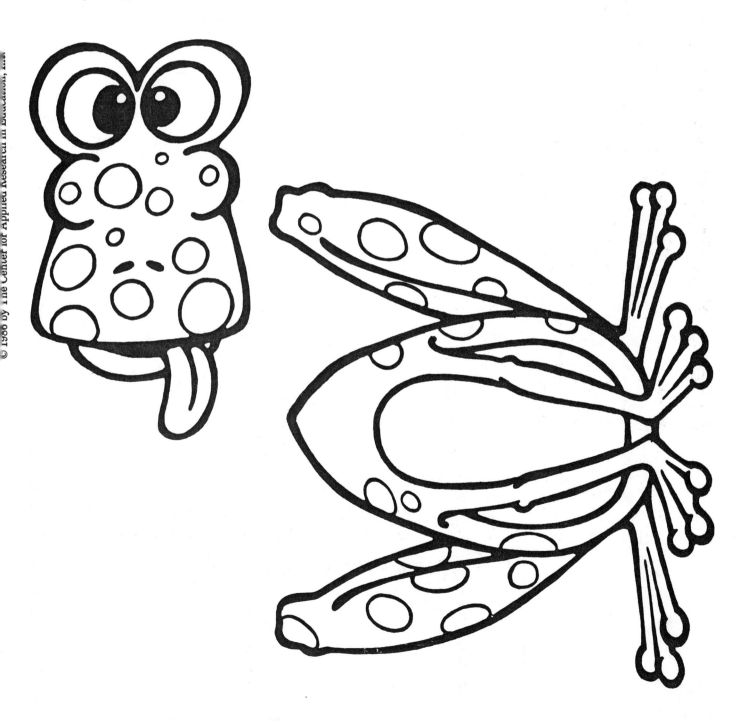

Name _____

Fill Fanny's Lunch Box

Fanny Frog is famished. She hasn't had a full meal in days! She can only eat flies that have **F** or **f** on them. Help Fanny fill her lunch box. Cut out the flies below that have **F** or **f** on them and stack them inside her lunch box. Fanny thinks you're fantastic!

Name _____

Fanny's Fishing Game (For 2 players)

One of Fanny's favorite free-time activities is fishing! To make Fanny's fishing game, here's what you do:

1. Glue the fish below and those on page Ff-4 onto pieces of heavy construction paper. Let them dry.
2. Cut out the fish on the black lines.
3. Tape a paper clip to each fish's mouth.
4. To make a fishing pole, tie a 2-foot-long piece of string to a small branch and the other end to a small magnet.

To play Fanny's fishing game, follow these directions:

1. Spread out the fish face down on the floor.
2. The first player casts the fishing pole into the "pond" and reels in a fish. He or she must name the **F** picture on the fish if there is one.
3. The second player takes a turn in the same way.
4. When all of the fish have been caught, the player with the most **f** fish pictures wins.

Name _____

Name _____

F f Puzzle

To solve this puzzle, color all of the lower-case **f** spaces orange. Color all of the capital **F** spaces blue. What **f** picture did you find?

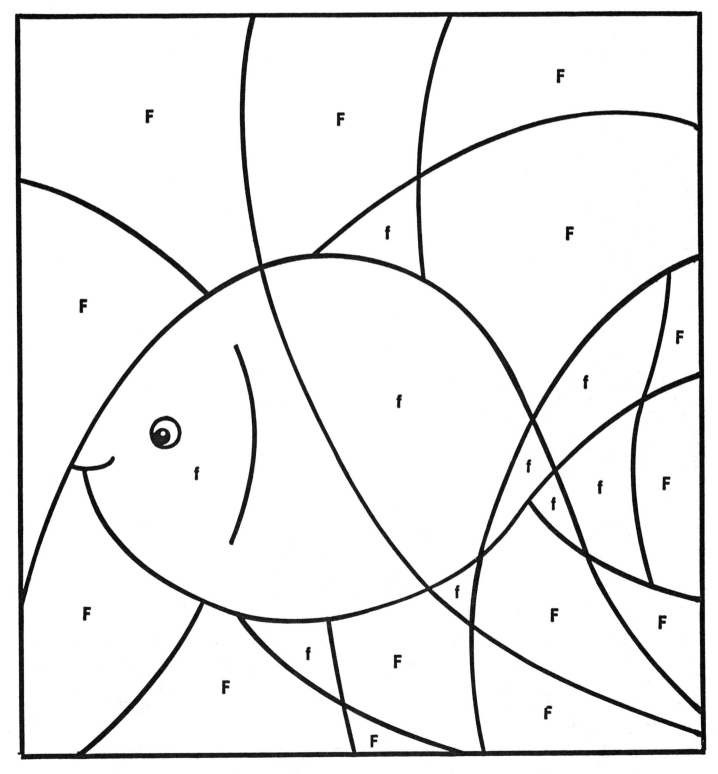

Name _____

Fanny Frog's Fudge (Serves 8–10)

You need:

1 12-ounce package carob or chocolate chips
40 marshmallows
½ cup butter
6 cups Rice Krispies

Directions:
Melt the carob (or chocolate) chips, marshmallows, and butter in a large pan over low heat. When these ingredients have melted, pour in the Rice Krispies. Take the pan off the burner and mix all of the ingredients with a spoon. Let the mixture cool for a few minutes. On a piece of waxed paper pour small amounts of fudge spaced apart. You can shape each piece into something starting with the **f** sound—like **fish** or **five!**

Name _____

D E F Letter Review

Practice writing these letters on the lines below. You have mastered the letters **D**, **d**, **E**, **e**, **F**, **f**. Congratulations!

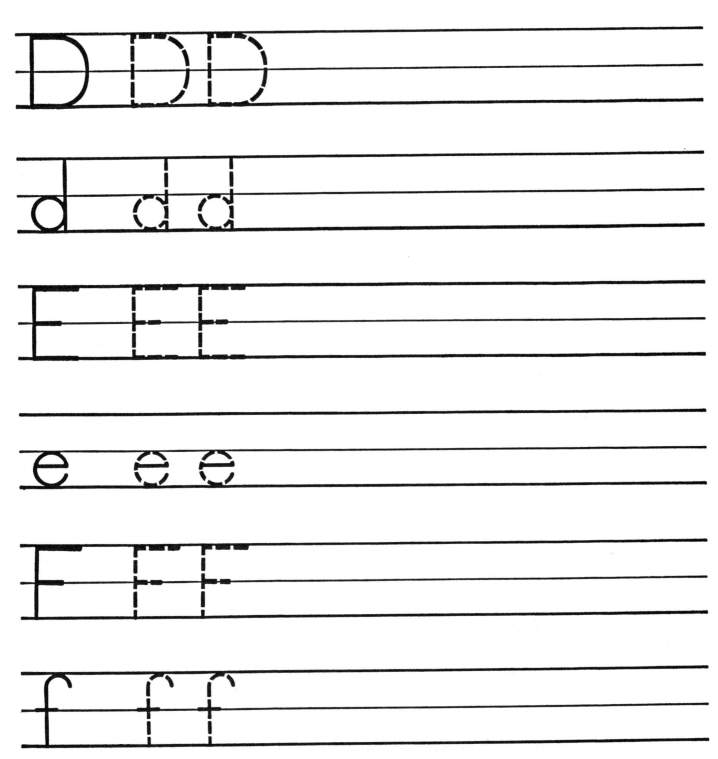

Finger Tracing the Letters G g

Reproduce this page for each child in your class. Have each child cut along the dotted line and discard the teacher directions. Then help each one glue gold glitter or colored gumdrops on the heavy black lines using white glue and making sure not to cover up the direction arrows.

When the glue is dry, have each child trace over the letters using the first finger and following the directions indicated by the numbered arrows.

Place the finished letter sheet with the child's name on the back in a shoebox for each child and locate the boxes in a convenient place where the children can practice tracing the letters daily. This will help them remember the names of the letters and the correct way to form them.

Name _____

The Ghastly Ghost Tale

Once upon a time there was a great ghost family that lived in Georgia. Mr. and Mrs. Gates often played games with their children, Gary, Gail, Gertrude, and Garth. They were a happy family and the children were well behaved except for what happened this one ghastly night.

On the night before Halloween, Mr. and Mrs. Gates wanted to visit a friend. They asked Gary and Gail, the two oldest children, to babysit for the others while they were gone. Mrs. Gates had made a delicious meal of all white foods to make sure her children would be sparkling white for Halloween the next night. She warned them not to eat anything but white foods or terrible things could happen.

After their parents left, the Gates children began to snack. They decided they weren't going to eat only white foods and they looked around for some other things to eat:

Big brother Gary found a bowl of garbanzo beans on the counter. Big sister Gail found a jar of gooseberry jelly in the refrigerator. Little sister Gertrude found some leftover goulash. And baby brother Garth found a stick of strawberry gum. They all started munching.

Suddenly Gary turned yellow, Gail became purple, Gertrude had brown splotches all over her, and Garth turned bright pink!

They were a gruesome sight when their parents came home that night! Color the Gates children the way they looked after their snacks. (Mrs. Gates gave them lots of white milk to turn them white again for Halloween!)

Name _____

The Gates' House

The Gates children are eager to go home after a busy night of ghostly pranks. They love their home and they need some sleep. But the only way they can enter or leave their home is when a **g** object appears at the window. Help the children get into their home. Here's what you do:

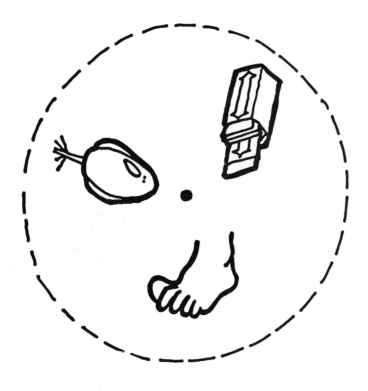

1. Cut out the window along the dotted lines in the house on page Gg-3.
2. Cut out the door on 3 sides along the dotted lines. Then fold back the door on the solid dark line.
3. Cut out the wheels on this page and attach one wheel to the back of the house with a paper brad. The pictures should show through the window. You can put on a new wheel whenever you like.
4. Turn the wheel until a **g** object appears in the window. Then the Gates children can come home.

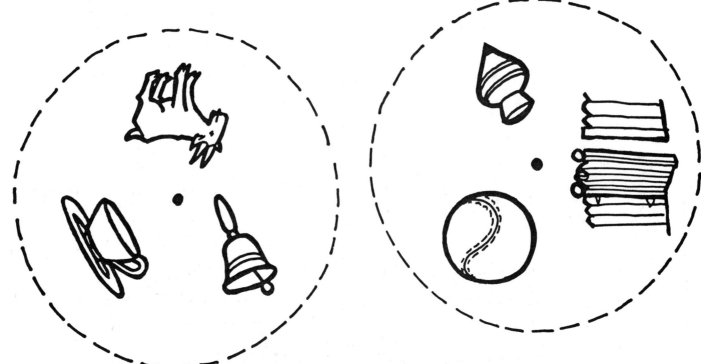

Name _____

To make each of the Gates children, stuff a small ball of tissue into the middle of a flat tissue. Tie under the ball with white thread to form a head. Make eyes, nose, and mouth with a marker.

Name _____

The Gates' Ghostly Glider

To make the Gates' ghostly glider, here's what you do:

1. Draw and color designs on the glider wings and center.
2. Cut out the glider along the dotted lines at the top and solid outside lines at the sides and bottom.
3. Fold under at the solid lines where they come to a point. Fold in at the center line so that the **g's** touch. Fold down the wings. Now glide!

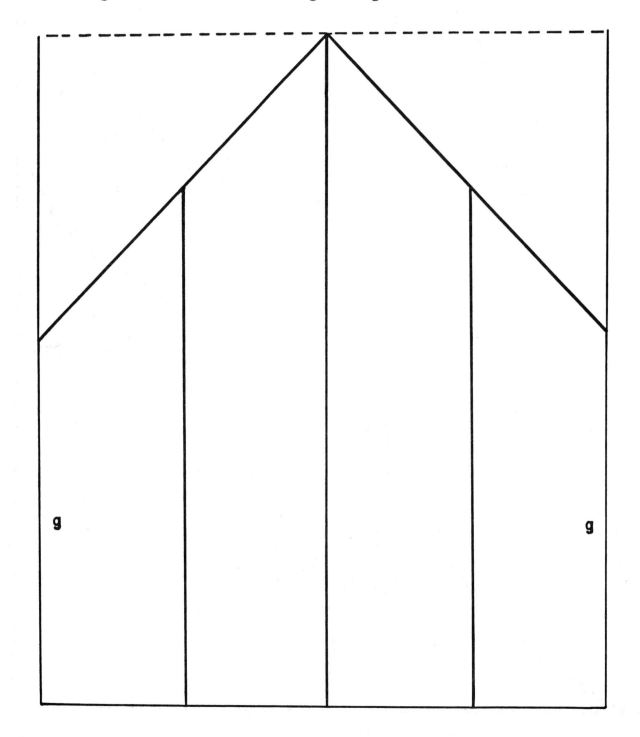

Name _____

G g Puzzle

To solve this puzzle, color the capital **G** spaces gray. Color the lower-case **g** spaces light blue. What **g** picture did you find?

Name _____

The Gates' Granola Gorp
(Serves 12)

You need:

2 cups granola cereal
1 cup peanuts
1 cup raisins
1 cup sunflower seeds
1 cup carob chips

Directions:
Place all of the ingredients into a large bowl. Carefully mix with a spoon. Store the "gorp" in an airtight container and enjoy it for a snack!

Finger Tracing the Letters H h

Reproduce this page for each child in your class. Have each child cut along the dotted line and discard the teacher directions. Then help each one glue "hair" (made of yarn) or hay on the heavy black lines using white glue and making sure not to cover up the direction arrows.

When the glue is dry, have each child trace over the letters using the first finger and following the directions indicated by the numbered arrows.

Place the finished letter sheet with the child's name on the back in a shoebox for each child and locate the boxes in a convenient place where the children can practice tracing the letters daily. This will help them remember the names of the letters and the correct way to form them.

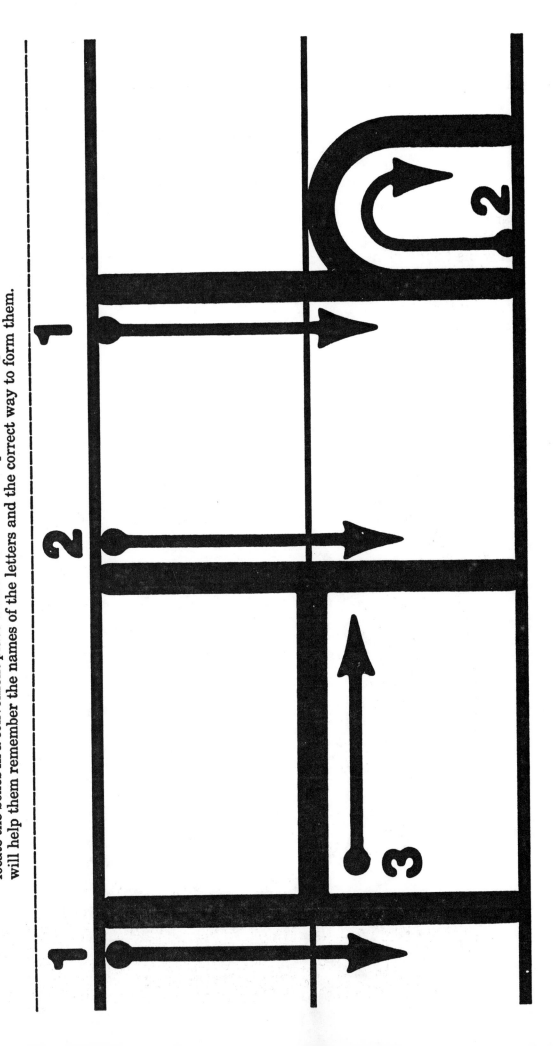

Name _____

Happy Harry's Hair

Happy Harry is usually a hilariously happy fellow. However, one day he had a horrible thing happen to him at the hamburger stand he owns. He was playing his harmonica very happily when his hair suddenly fell out! This made Harry very unhappy. Help him by giving him some new hair. Cut and glue yarn on Harry's head and then draw his happy grin!

Name _____

Happy Harry's Hats

Color Happy Harry's hats, cut them out, and try
them on his picture on page Hh-1. Then make more
of your own hats for Harry.

Name _____

Happy Harry's Hamburger Game
(For 2 players)

To play Happy Harry's hamburger game, here's what you do:

1. Glue pages Hh-3 and Hh-4 to a piece of heavy construction paper and let them dry.
2. Cut out the hamburger buns and patties on this page, and cut out the patties on the dotted lines. Cut out 2 sets of the cards on page Hh-4.
3. Shuffle the cards and place them in a stack face down.
4. The first player tosses a penny in the air. If it lands face up, he or she gets to choose a card from the stack. If the penny does not land face up, play goes to the next player.
5. When a player picks a picture card from the top of the stack, he or she must name it correctly and place it at the bottom of the stack. If correct, he or she picks another card. If not, play goes to the next player.
6. When a player gets a card with instructions, he or she takes the piece to make a hamburger and play goes to the next player. The first person to make a complete hamburger (2 buns and a whole patty) is the winner.

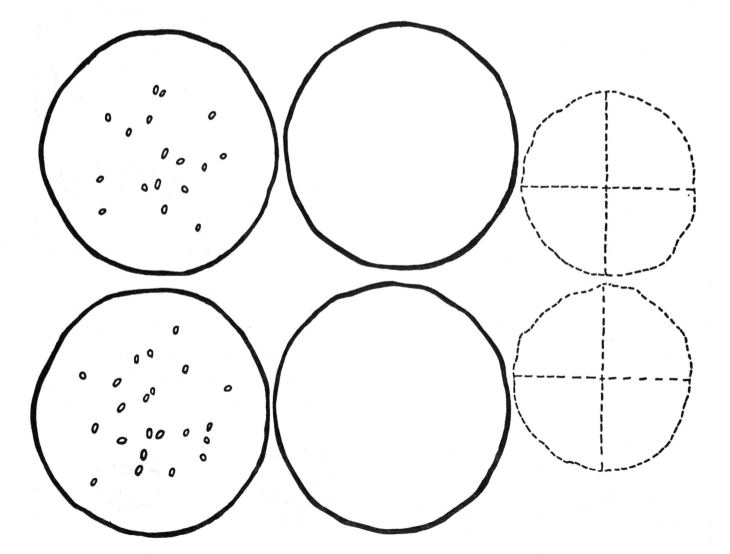

Name _____

Take the top bun for your hamburger.	Take ¼ of a hamburger patty.	Take ¼ of a hamburger patty.	Take the bottom bun for your hamburger.
Take the top bun for your hamburger.	Take ¼ of a hamburger patty.	Take ¼ of a hamburger patty.	Take the bottom bun for your hamburger.

Name _____

Match Harry's Animal Friends and Foods

Happy Harry has animal friends who like foods other than hamburger. Help Harry's friends get something to eat by drawing a line from each animal to the food you think it would like.

Name _____

H h Puzzle

To solve this puzzle, color the lower-case **h** spaces light brown. Color the *empty* spaces light yellow. What **h** picture did you find?

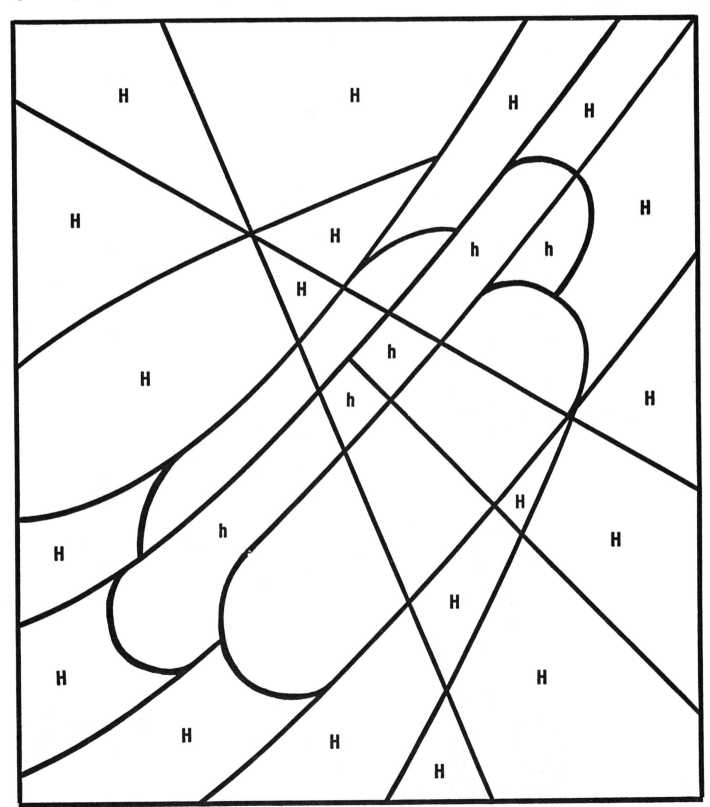

Name _____

Happy Harry's Hamburgers (Serves 4)

You need:

1 pound hamburger
1 8-ounce can crushed pineapple
4 hamburger buns

Directions:
Place the hamburger and drained pineapple into a bowl and mix thoroughly with clean hands. Divide the mixture into 4 parts and shape each into a patty. Cook the patties on a grill or in a frying pan until they are done. Place each patty on a bun and add whatever toppings you like.

Finger Tracing the Letters I i

Reproduce this page for each child in your class. Have each child cut along the dotted line and discard the teacher directions. Then help each one glue "icicles" (Christmas tinsel) or pieces of **crushed ice cream cone** on the heavy black lines using white glue and making sure not to cover up the direction arrows.

When the glue is dry, have each child trace over the letters using the first finger and following the directions indicated by the numbered arrows.

Place the finished letter sheet with the child's name on the back in a shoebox for each child and locate the boxes in a convenient place where the children can practice tracing the letters daily. This will help them remember the names of the letters and the correct way to form them.

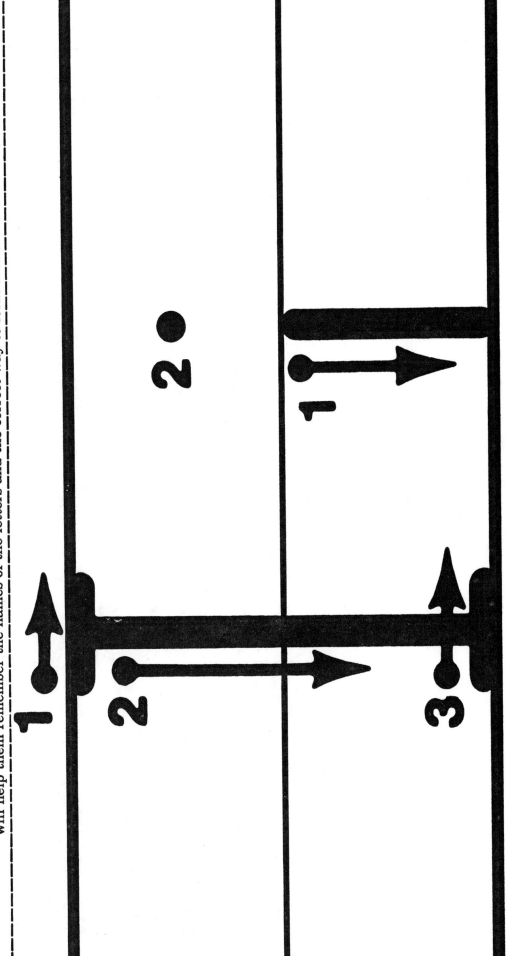

Name _____

Ichabod Iguana

Ichabod is supposed to eat insects like all good iguanas, but he thinks they're icky! All he can think about eating is ice cream. He loves every flavor you can imagine. Color Ichabod's ice cream for the flavors you think he likes best.

Name _____

Help Ichabod Eat Ice Cream Cones

On this page and page Ii-3 color and cut out Ichabod's face and only the ice cream cones with **i** pictures on them. Make circles of tape with the sticky side out and put one on each **i** ice cream cone and on Ichabod. Tape Ichabod to a wall (with your teacher's permission). Have someone blindfold you, spin you around 3 times, and face you toward Ichabod. Then see how close you can place Ichabod's ice cream cones to his mouth!

Name _____

Name _____

Match Ichabod's Friends

As you know, Ichabod would much rather eat ice cream than insects. He has made friends with many of the insects near his home. Circle his two insect friends on this page that are exactly alike. Then color all the insects.

Name _____

I i Puzzle

To solve this puzzle, color the capital **I** spaces black. Color the lower-case **i** spaces light blue. What **i** picture did you find?

Name _____

Ichabod's Ice Cream (Serves 16)

You need:

4 cups whipping cream
1 cup powdered sugar
2 tablespoons vanilla
¼ teaspoon salt
4 egg whites
fruit, nuts, or flavorings (peaches, apricots, bananas, strawberries, raspberries, peppermint stick candy, chocolate syrup, pistachio nuts, orange juice, or whatever you like)

Directions:
With an electric beater (**caution**) beat the whipping cream until stiff. Sift the powdered sugar into the cream and then add the vanilla. Mix well. Add salt to the egg whites and whip until frothy. Fold the egg mixture into the cream mixture, then fold in fruit, nuts, or flavorings of your choice. Pour the mixture into shallow trays, cover with plastic wrap, and freeze until mushy. Whip the partially frozen mixture with the beater, then return to the freezer until firm.

Name _____

G H I Letter Review

Practice writing these letters on the lines below. You have mastered the letters G, g, H, h, I, i. Congratulations!

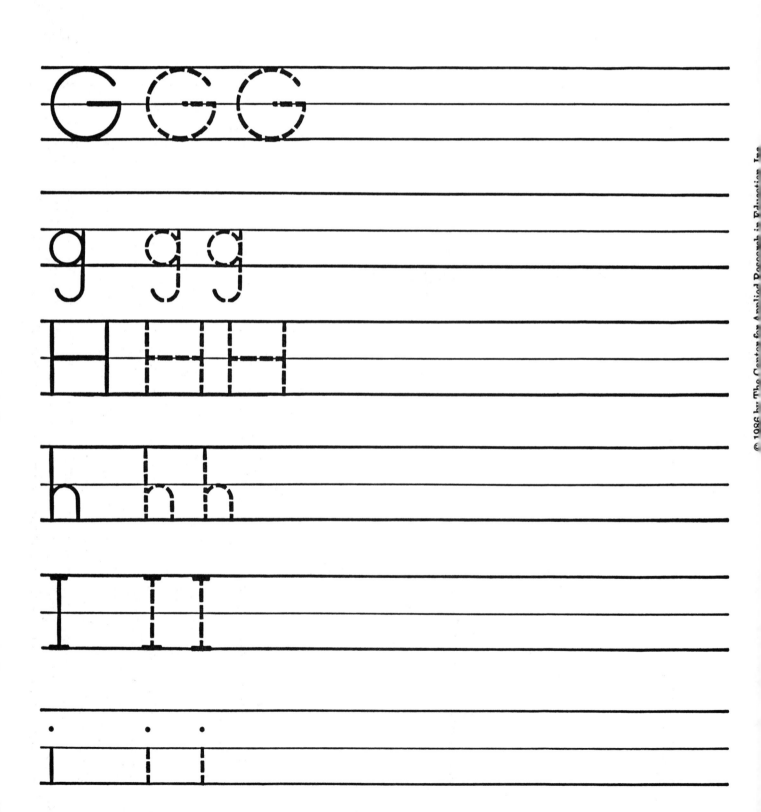

Finger Tracing the Letters J j

Reproduce this page for each child in your class. Have each child cut along the dotted line and discard the teacher directions. Then help each one glue small jellybeans on the heavy black lines using white glue and making sure not to cover up the direction arrows.

When the glue is dry, have each child trace over the letters using the first finger and following the directions indicated by the numbered arrows.

Place the finished letter sheet with the child's name on the back in a shoebox for each child and locate the boxes in a convenient place where the children can practice tracing the letters daily. This will help them remember the names of the letters and the correct way to form them.

Name _____

Jumping Jack

My name is Jack and I live in New Jersey. My friend James and I were driving along in a jeep one day when I suddenly fell out! To help put me back together again, here's what you do:

1. Color and cut out all of my pieces.
2. Accordion fold the long strip.
3. Glue yarn on my head.
4. Glue the hat to the top of my head.
5. Glue the box to a piece of plain paper and glue the folded strip to the top of the box.
6. Glue my head onto the top of the folded paper. Let me dry for several hours.
7. Now gently press me down into my box and see me jump up!

Name _____

What Comes Next?

When Jack isn't eating jellybeans or jumping around, he enjoys working in his garden. Help tell a story about Jack's garden. Here's what you do:

1. Look at the first three pictures at the top of the page.
2. Find a picture below the dotted line that will complete the story.
3. Cut out the picture that will finish the story and glue it into the empty box.
4. Color the story pictures.

Name _____

Junk Printing

To make a junk printing, here's what you do:

1. Collect various junk items that have interesting shapes and textures, like bottle caps, aluminum cans, lids, leaves, toothbrushes, sponges.
2. Pour several colors of thick tempera paint into different bowls.
3. Dip each junk item into a different color and press onto the paper below. Use your imagination to create an interesting picture!
4. Another time you can use household items to make a picture. Collect cookie cutters, a potato masher or pastry brush, forks, spoons, table knives, a wire whisk, a cheese grater, and other items to dip into paint and press onto paper.

Name _____

Jack's J Game (For 2 players)

To play Jack's J game, follow these directions:

1. Cut out the J gameboard and glue it to a piece of heavy paper or cardboard.
2. Place the gameboard on a smooth floor.
3. The first player stands directly over the gameboard and drops a penny from waist height. If the penny lands in a space, the player names the **j** picture, and gets the point in the circle in that space if he or she is correct. Then the second player takes a turn.
4. If the penny lands on a line or off the gameboard, the player takes turns until it lands in a **j** space.
5. The first player to earn 10 points is the winner!

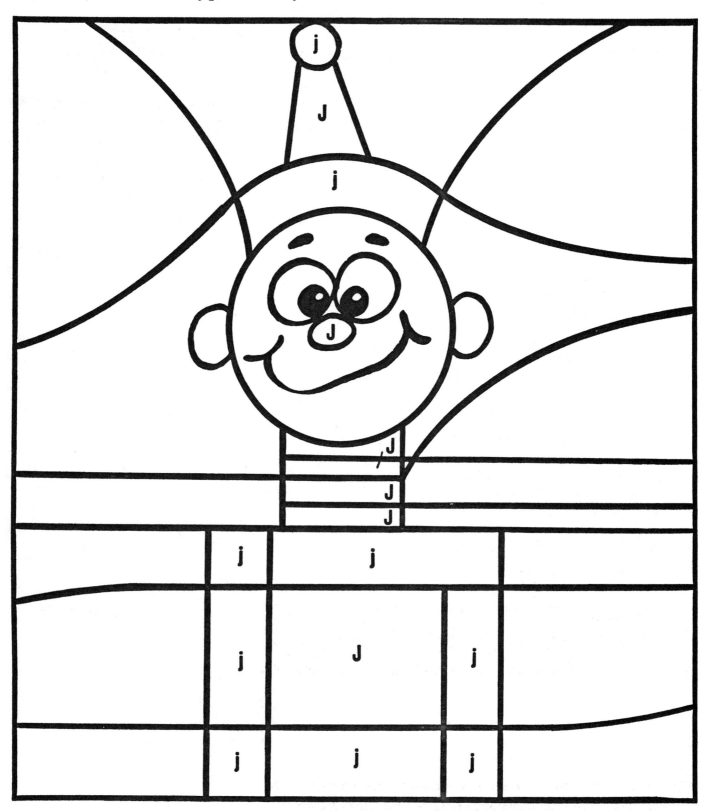

Name _____

J j Puzzle

To solve this puzzle, color the capital **J** spaces red and color the lower-case **j** spaces any color you like. What **j** picture did you find?

Name _____

Jumping Jack's Jell-O
(Serves 8–10)

You need:

3 3-ounce packages of Jell-O in different flavors
4 envelopes unflavored gelatin
1 cup sugar (*optional*)
5 cups boiling water
1½ teaspoons lemon juice

Directions:
IMPORTANT: This recipe makes 3 separate layers, so you will need to make the following 3 separate times, once for each flavor.

Place 1 package Jell-O, 1-1/3 envelopes unflavored gelatin, and 1/3 cup sugar in a bowl. Add 1-2/3 cups boiling water (**with caution**). Stir well with a wooden spoon. Stir in ½ teaspoon lemon juice. Pour the mixture into a 4-quart baking dish. Let it stand in the **refrigerator** for several hours until firm. Repeat this recipe for 2 more layers and let the mold set overnight. Cut it into small wedges and enjoy!

Finger Tracing the Letters K k

Reproduce this page for each child in your class. Have each child cut along the dotted line and discard the teacher directions. Then help each one trace on the heavy black lines using **ketchup** (and wearing a smock), making sure not to cover up the direction arrows.

When the ketchup is dry, have each child trace over the letters using the first finger and following the directions indicated by the numbered arrows.

Place the finished letter sheet with the child's name on the back in a shoebox for each child and locate the boxes in a convenient place where the children can practice tracing the letters daily. This will help them remember the names of the letters and the correct way to form them.

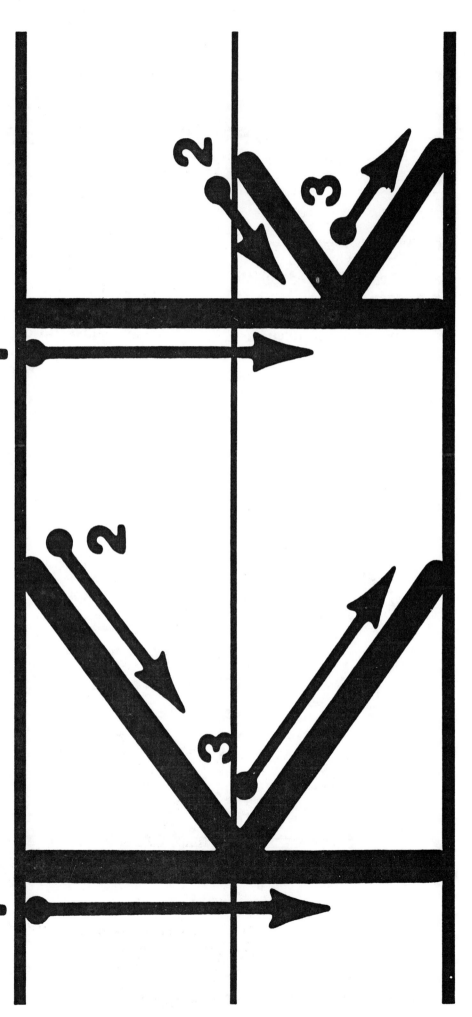

© 1986 by The Center for Applied Research in Education, Inc.

Name _____

Kelly Kangaroo

Kelly Kangaroo is going to visit her cousin Kristen in Kansas. She is taking along some presents to give to her friends, but she can only take presents with the **k** sound. Help Kelly load the presents in her pouch. Color Kelly and cut her pouch on the dotted line, then find her **k** presents on page Kk-2.

Name _____

K Presents for Kelly's Trip

Cut out the pouch pocket and put a line of white glue along the edges. Glue the pocket to the back of Kelly Kangaroo's pouch. Let dry. Color and cut out the **k** presents for Kelly to take on her trip. Then draw 3 more **k** presents of your own and color them. Place all of the **k** presents into Kelly's pouch so she can be on her way!

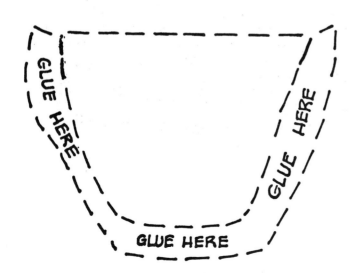

Name _____

Find the K Things

In this kitchen picture there are 4 things that begin with the **k** sound. Color each **k** thing you find.

Name _____

K k Puzzle

To solve this puzzle, color the capital **K** spaces gold. What **k** picture did you find?

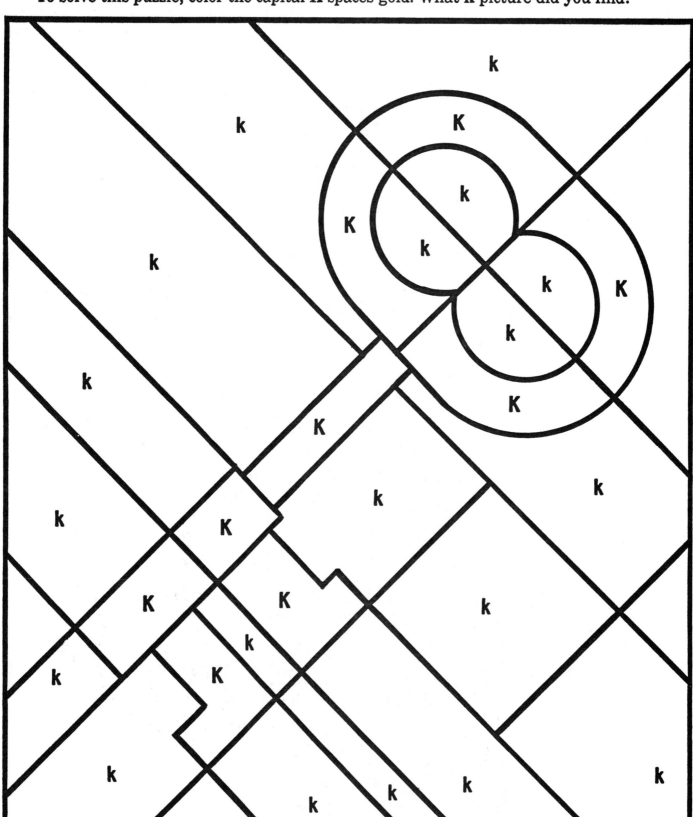

Name _____

2 children

Kelly's Kebabs

You need:

fruits that can be cut in chunks or
can be used whole, such as:
- apples (cut)
- peaches (cut)
- pineapple (cut)
- bananas (thickly sliced)
- maraschino cherries
- grapes
- melon (cut)
- pears (cut)
- (canned fruit can also be used)

Directions:
Place the fruit one piece at a time on small skewers or long toothpicks. Place different fruits next to one another and vary the colors, too.

Finger Tracing the Letters L l

Reproduce this page for each child in your class. Have each child cut along the dotted line and discard the teacher directions. Then help each one glue strips of lace on the heavy black lines using white glue and making sure not to cover up the direction arrows.

When the glue is dry, have each child trace over the letters using the first finger and following the directions indicated by the numbered arrows.

Place the finished letter sheet with the child's name on the back in a shoebox for each child and locate the boxes in a convenient place where the children can practice tracing the letters daily. This will help them remember the names of the letters and the correct way to form them.

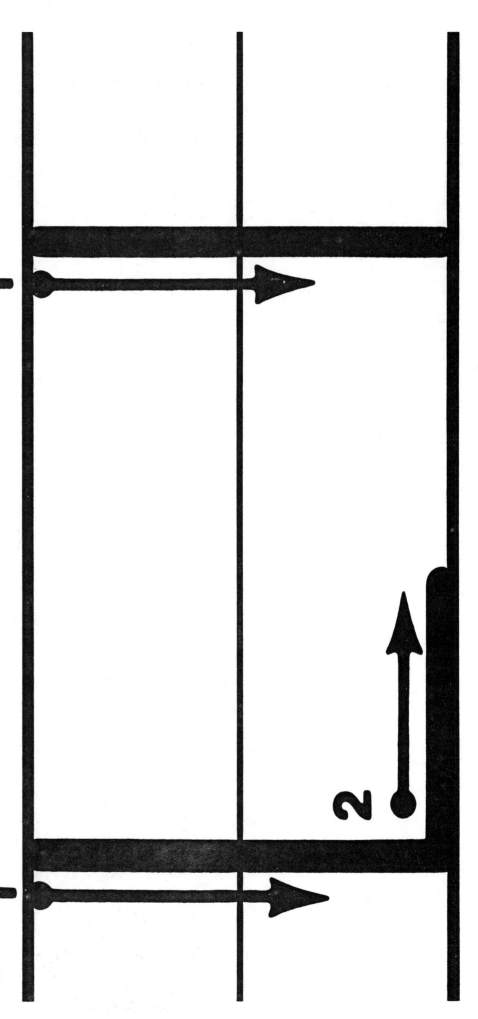

Name _____

Leonard Lion Puppet

Leonard the lion loves lollipops! He's traveled as far as Louisiana for a few licks. Help put Leonard together so he can live with you. Here's what you do:

1. Color Leonard light yellow, then cut out his head and body.
2. Glue a mixture of yellow and brown yarn all around the backside of his head to form a mane.
3. Glue Leonard's head to the bottom flap of a paper lunch bag. Make sure the part of the bag that folds over is under his chin.
4. Glue Leonard's body onto the bag under the fold.

Name _____

Leonard's Friend Launi

Leonard the lion has a ladybug friend whose name is Launi. Leonard and Launi like to lounge around most of the day. Help put Launi together so Leonard won't be lonely. Here's what you do:

1. Color Launi's spots black.
2. Color the rest of her wings and her body red.
3. Cut out Launi's body and wings.
4. Overlap the wings at the small black dots and put a paper brad through the dots.
5. Put the paper brad through Launi's body at point L. Flatten the brad on the underside of her body.

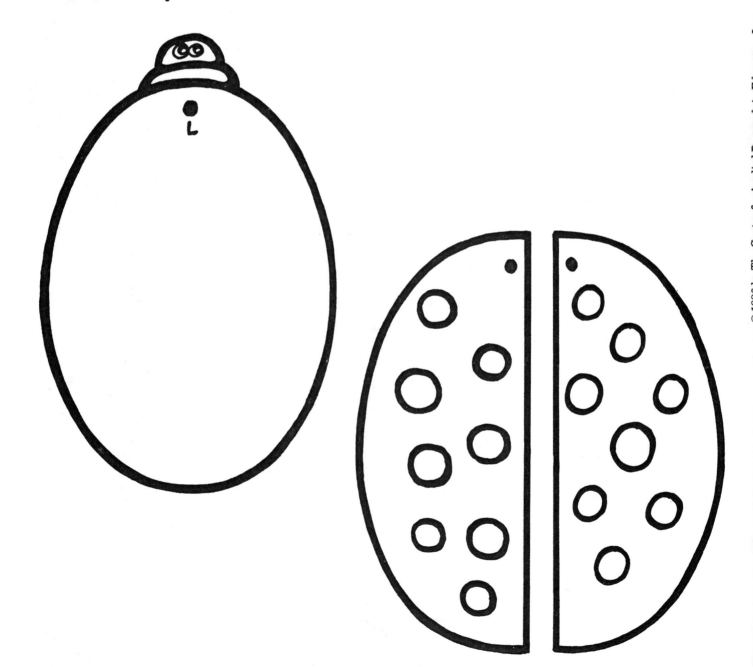

Name _____

Leonard's Lemon Lollipops

Leonard and Launi found some lemon lollipops in a store in Louisiana. Help them decorate the lollipops. Here's what you do:

1. Color each lollipop lemon yellow.
2. Cut out magazine pictures of things that start with the l sound.
3. Glue the pictures onto Leonard's and Launi's lemon lollipops.

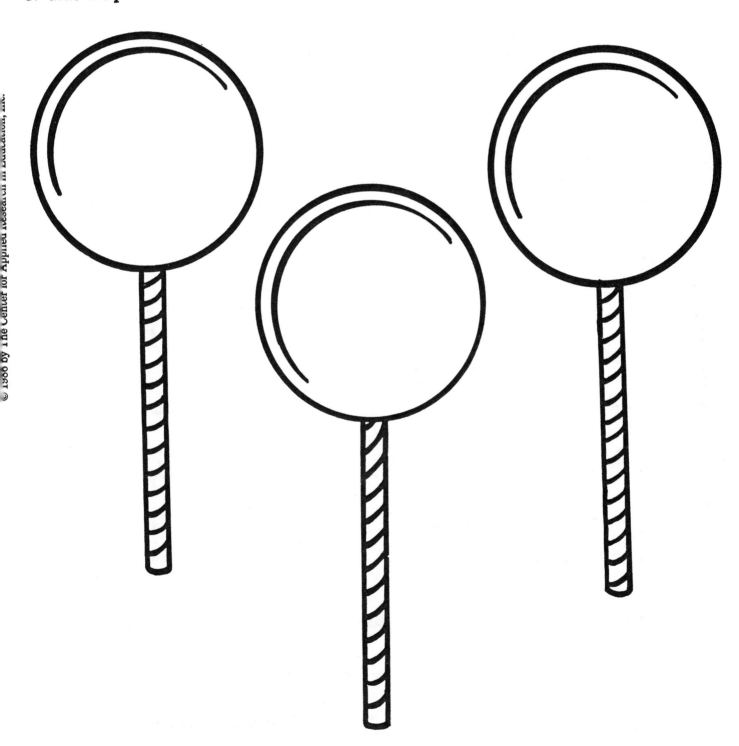

Name _____

Match Leonard's Lollipops

Leonard was lounging around the local candy shop one day. He wanted to buy two lollipops that looked the same for himself and Launi. Help Leonard by coloring the two lollipops in the store window that are exactly the same.

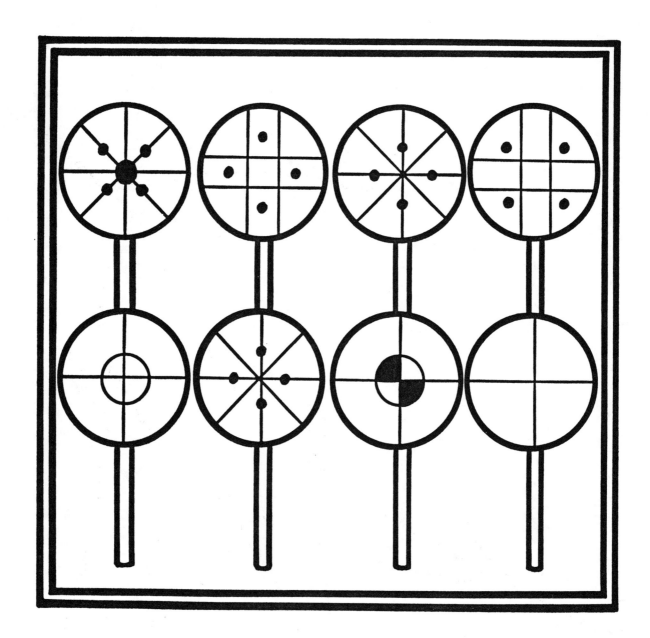

Name _____

L l Puzzle

To solve this puzzle, color the lower-case **l** spaces green. What **l** picture did you find?

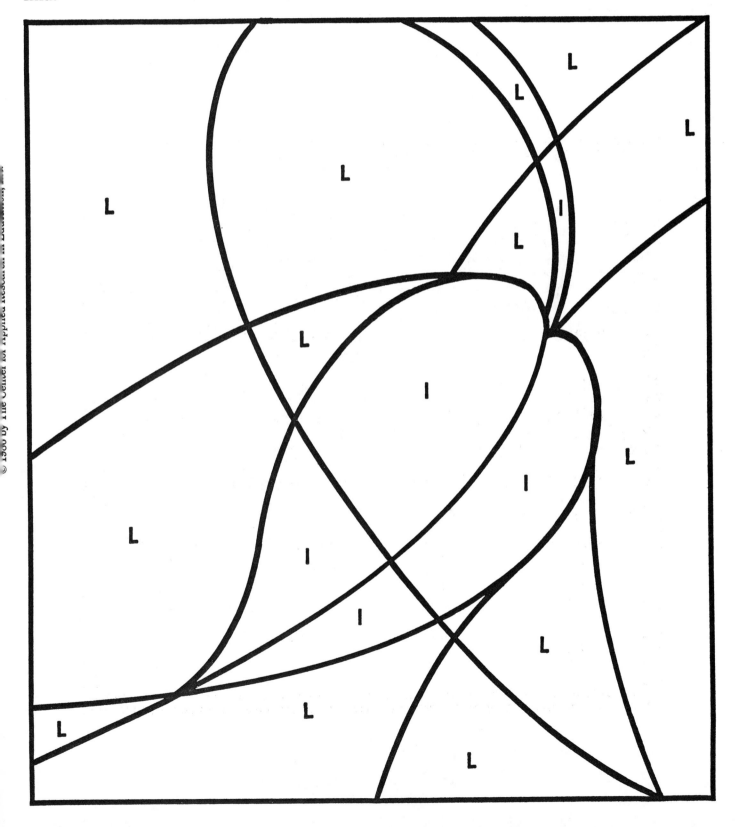

Name _____

Leonard's Lemon Pie (Serves 8)

You need:

3 8-ounce cartons lemon yogurt
1 8-ounce container nondairy
  whipped topping
1 9" deep-dish baked pie shell

Directions:
Gently fold the lemon yogurt into the whipped topping with a spoon in a large bowl. Pour this mixture into a baked pie shell, cover with plastic wrap, and place in the freezer for one hour. Then slice and enjoy!

Name _____

J K L Letter Review

Practice writing these letters on the lines below. You have mastered the letters J, j, K, k, L, l. Congratulations!

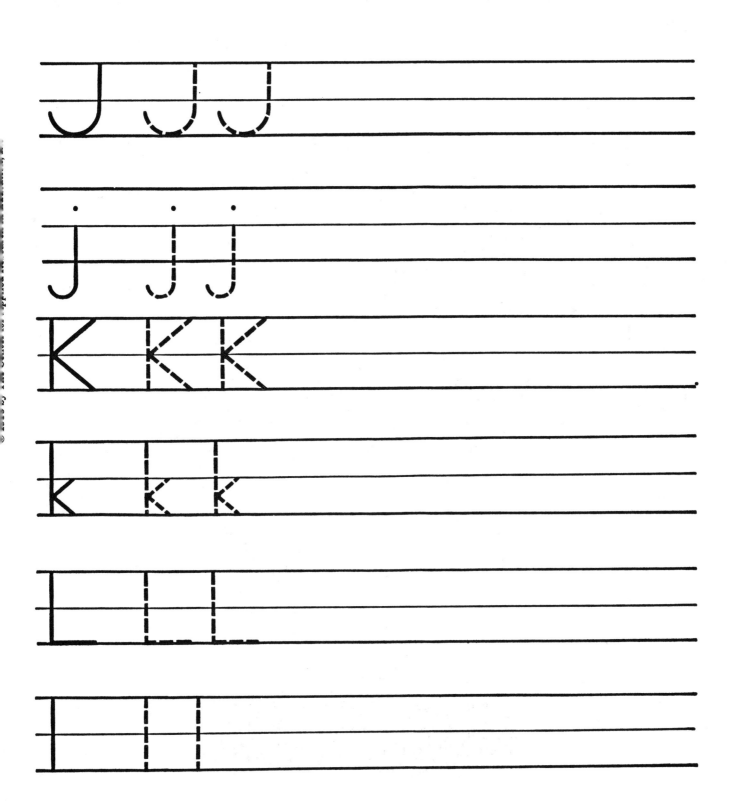

Finger Tracing the Letters M m

Reproduce this page for each child in your class. Have each child cut along the dotted line and discard the teacher directions. Then help each one glue macaroni or miniature marshmallows on the heavy black lines using white glue and making sure not to cover up the direction arrows.

When the glue is dry, have each child trace over the letters using the first finger and following the directions indicated by the numbered arrows.

Place the finished letter sheet with the child's name on the back in a shoebox for each child and locate the boxes in a convenient place where the children can practice tracing the letters daily. This will help them remember the names of the letters and the correct way to form them.

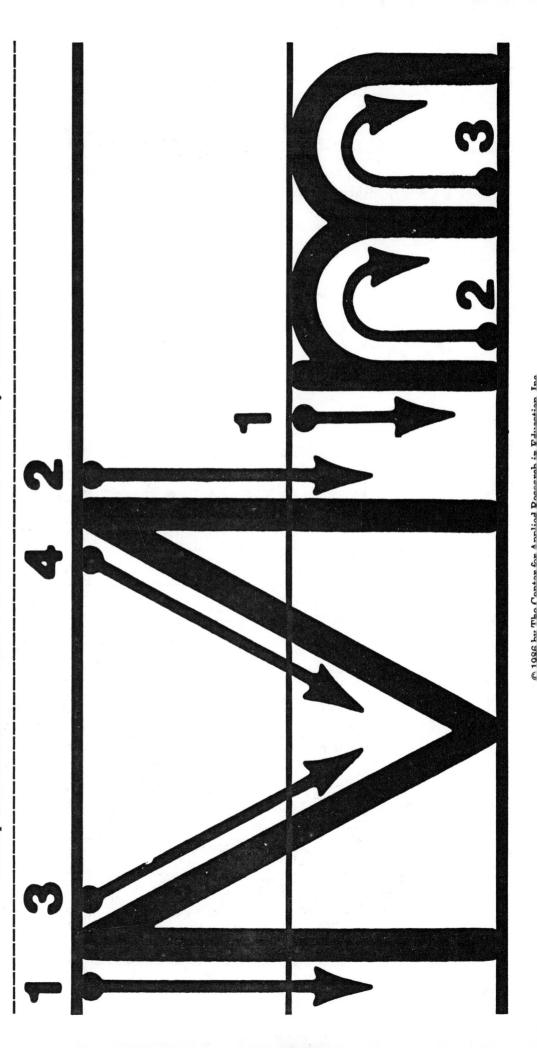

Name _____

Matthew and Melinda Mouse

Matthew and Melinda Mouse were recently married in Michigan. The minister, Mr. Miller, performed the ceremony in May. Help Matthew and Melinda replace their missing tails. Glue yarn or pipe cleaners where their tails should go, then color the rest of the picture.

Name _____

Matthew and Melinda's Meal

Matthew and Melinda Mouse have been traveling to Montana on their honeymoon. They are very hungry, but they haven't had time to munch on some morsels of food. They can only eat foods that begin with the **m** sound. Help the mice by cutting out **m** foods in magazines and gluing them on this plate. Their tummies will feel marvelous. Yum!

Name _____

Magic Marble Painting

To paint a marvelous way with marbles, here's what you do:

1. Cut out the circle on this page and also cut out the small circle in the center.
2. Trace the small circle 4 times on another piece of paper and cut out all circles.
3. Place one small circle in the bottom of a pie pan.
4. Dip 2 marbles each in a different color of tempera paint.
5. Place the marbles in the pan and roll them around on the paper. The marbles will leave an interesting pattern trail.
6. Repeat these steps on the 3 other circles and choose the one you like best.
7. When it is dry, place it inside the large circle and glue the pieces to another sheet of paper.

Name _____

M m Puzzle

To solve this puzzle, color the capital M spaces black. What m picture did you find?

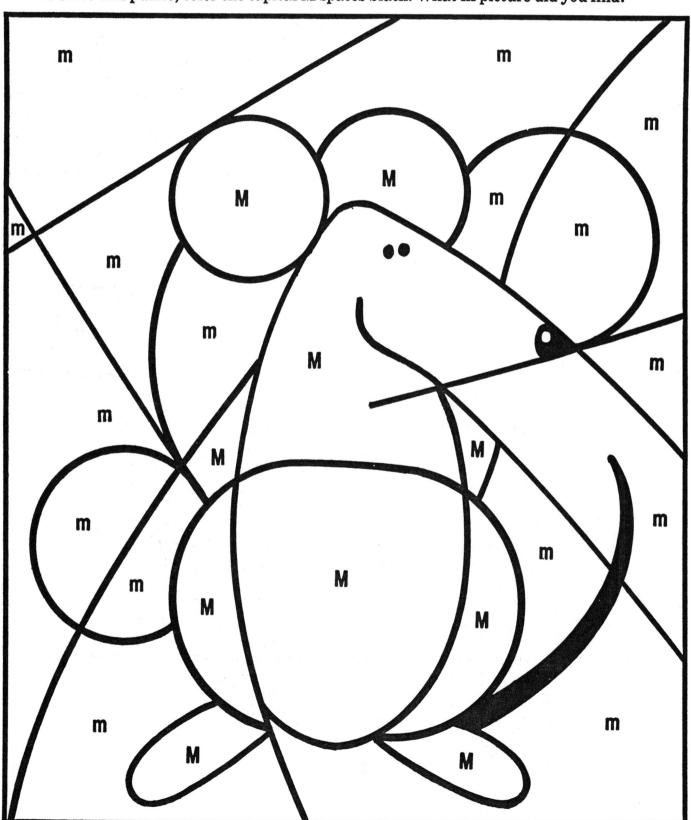

Name _____

Matthew and Melinda's Marvelous Muffins
(Serves 6)

You need:

1¾ cup whole wheat flour
2 teaspoons double-acting baking
  powder
2 eggs
⅓ cup honey
¼ cup melted butter
¾ cup milk
1 cup fresh blueberries

Directions:
Sift the flour and baking powder together into a large bowl. Beat the eggs with a table fork in a small bowl. Then add the melted butter and milk to the eggs and mix. Pour the egg mixture into the flour mixture and stir well with a wooden spoon. Gently fold in the blueberries. Pour the muffin mixture into a greased muffin tin and bake in a 400° oven for 20 to 25 minutes. Enjoy them while they're warm!

Finger Tracing the Letters N n

Reproduce this page for each child in your class. Have each child cut along the dotted line and discard the teacher directions. Then help each child glue dried noodles in several shapes on the heavy black lines using white glue and making sure not to cover up the direction arrows.

When the glue is dry, have each child trace over the letters using the first finger and following the directions indicated by the numbered arrows.

Place the finished letter sheet with the child's name on the back in a shoebox for each child and locate the boxes in a convenient place where the children can practice tracing the letters daily. This will help them remember the names of the letters and the correct way to form them.

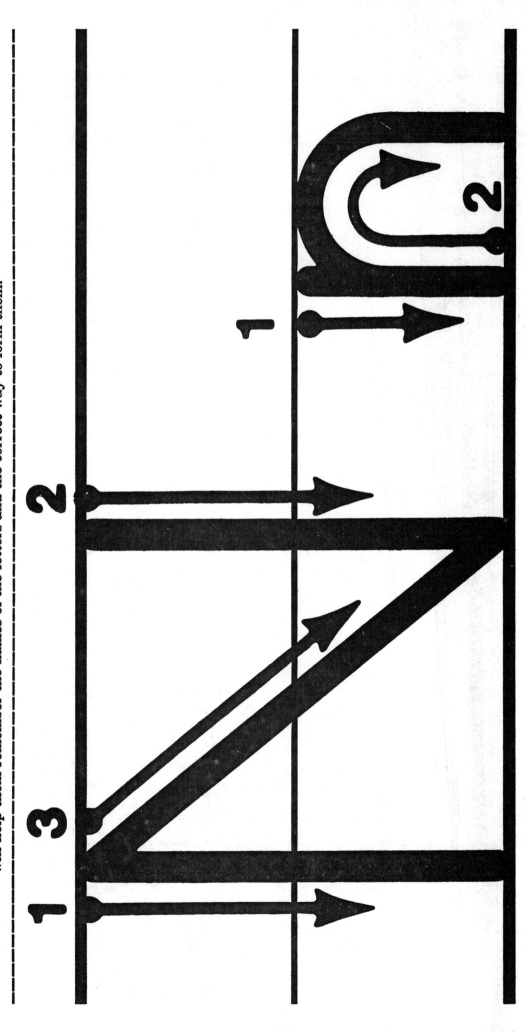

Name _____

Neil and Nancy

Neil and Nancy are neighbors in New Mexico. They will soon be attending a new school, and their parents bought them some nifty new clothes. Help Neil and Nancy get ready for school. Color and cut out the kids and their clothes. Dress them, then think of places that begin with the sound of **n** to which they could go after school.

Name _____

Make a Necktie for Your Neighbor

To make a necktie for your neighbor, here s wnat you do:

1. Glue this page to a piece of heavy construction paper. Let dry.
2. Color or paint the neckties and let dry.
3. Cut out the neckties. Punch two holes with a hole puncher through the small dots in the center of each tie.
4. Thread a 16″ piece of sewing elastic through the holes and tie the ends securely to fit around the neck.

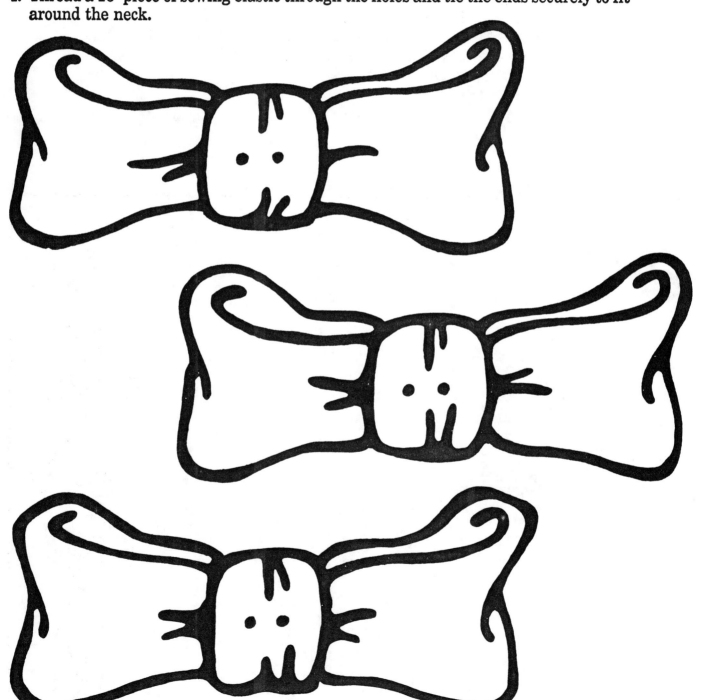

Name _____

N Matching Game (For 1 player)

To make and play the N matching game, here's what you do:

1. Glue each gameboard to heavy paper or cardboard. Let dry.
2. Cut out the gameboards.
3. Using a hole puncher, punch the hole next to the letters N n. Also punch a hole next to each picture on the right side of the board.
4. Cut 9 pieces of 9" yarn or string. Place 3 strings through each N n hole and tape the ends to the back of the gameboard.
5. To play the game, name each picture on the right side of the gameboard. Then string the yarn from the N n to those pictures that start with the **n** sound.

Name _____

N n ○

N n ○

Name _____

String a Noodle Necklace (Makes 4)

To make a noodle necklace for Mom or yourself, here's what you do:

1. Divide a 16-ounce package of small circular macaroni (tubettini) into 4 equal parts.
2. Pour ¼ cup of rubbing alcohol into a jar with a lid. Place 6 to 12 drops of food coloring into the alcohol.
3. Place ¼ of the macaroni into the jar. Place the lid on the jar tightly and shake until the macaroni is colored.
4. Drain off the alcohol and spread the macaroni onto paper towels to dry.
5. Repeat these steps to make three more colors of macaroni.
6. Thread a blunt needle with thick sewing thread or thin yarn. String the macaroni to the length you wish. Tie the ends securely.

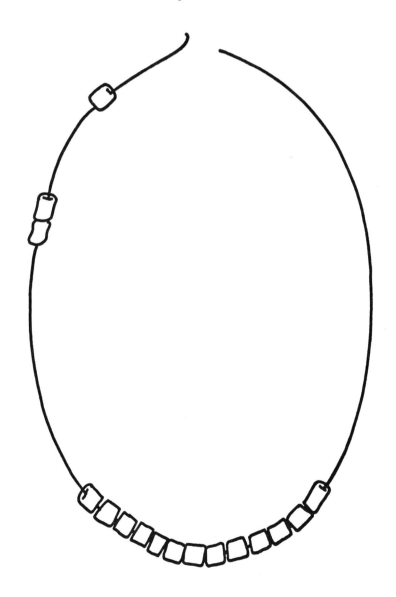

Name _____

N n Puzzle

To solve this puzzle, color the lower-case **n** spaces any color you would like. What **n** picture did you find?

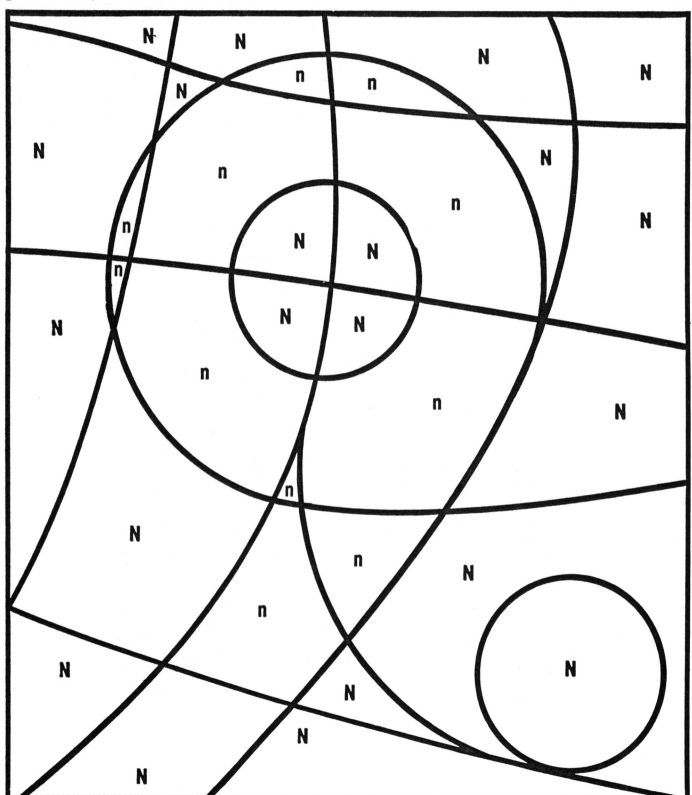

Name _____

Neil and Nancy's Noodles (Serves 8)

You need:

3 quarts boiling water
2 cups dry noodles
½ cup butter
1 8-ounce carton sour cream (*optional*)
¾ cup grated Parmesan cheese

Directions:
Carefully place the noodles into the boiling water (**use caution**). Boil gently 6 to 8 minutes or until tender. Melt the butter in a saucepan and mix in the sour cream and Parmesan cheese. Drain the noodles in a colander and place them in a bowl. Pour the cheese mixture over the noodles and toss the noodles gently with spoons until they are covered with the cheese mixture.

Finger Tracing the Letters O o

Reproduce this page for each child in your class. Have each child cut along the dotted line and discard the teacher directions. Then help each one glue Cheerios or dry oatmeal flakes on the heavy black lines using white glue and making sure not to cover up the direction arrows.

When the glue is dry, have each child trace over the letters using the first finger and following the directions indicated by the numbered arrows.

Place the finished letter sheet with the child's name on the back in a shoebox for each child and locate the boxes in a convenient place where the children can practice tracing the letters daily. This will help them remember the names of the letters and the correct way to form them.

Name _____

Olive Otter

Olive the otter is often seen with her friend Owen the octopus. They both like to search the ocean for unusual objects. Draw and color some unusual objects starting with the **o** sound that Olive and Owen might see in the ocean.

Name _____

Olive's O Picture Frame

Olive the otter would like a picture of you to show her ocean friends. To make this picture frame, here's what you do:

1. Glue this page to a sheet of heavy construction paper.
2. Cut out the O picture frame and also cut out the inside circle.
3. Decorate the frame with whatever you like — sequins, buttons, rickrack, tissue paper, seeds, ribbons, fall leaves.
4. Tape a picture of yourself to the back of the O frame.

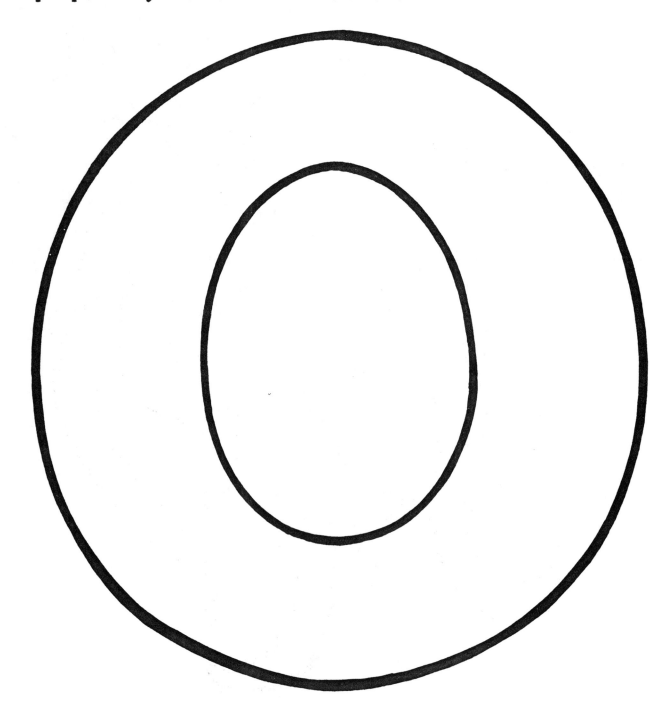

Name _____

Owen Octopus

Owen the Octopus would like to join your family. To make Owen, here's what you do:

1. Cut out Owen and glue him to a piece of blue paper for the ocean.
2. He needs his suckers to attach himself firmly to objects, so glue Cheerios to his tentacles.
3. Draw and color other sea life, then glue it to your picture.

Name _____

Olive's O Game (For 2 players)

You can play this thinking game with a friend. Here's what you do:

1. Glue the card sheet below onto a piece of heavy paper and let dry.
2. Cut out the cards, shuffle them, and spread them on a table face down.
3. The first player turns 2 cards face up to try to make a pair. If the cards match, he keeps them and the second player takes a turn. If they do not match, he turns them face down and the second player looks for a pair. The player with the most pairs of **o** cards wins.

Name _____

O o Puzzle

To solve this puzzle, color the capital **O** spaces brown. Color the lower-case **o** spaces light blue. What **o** picture did you find?

Name _____

Olive's Oatmeal Cookies (Serves 24)

You need:

½ cup brown sugar, firmly packed
⅓ cup honey
½ cup butter
1 egg
1 teaspoon vanilla
1 tablespoon milk
1 cup flour
½ teaspoon soda
½ teaspoon double-acting baking
   powder
1 cup uncooked rolled oats

Directions:
In a large bowl, combine the brown sugar, honey and butter with a wooden spoon until soft. In a separate bowl beat the egg, vanilla, and milk with a fork. Add the egg mixture to the sugar-butter mixture. Sift the flour, soda, and baking powder together into another bowl. Add the sugar mixture to the flour mixture and mix in the oats. With a spoon, drop cookies 2 inches apart on a well-greased cookie sheet. Bake the cookies in a 350° oven for 10 to 13 minutes.

Name _____

M N O Letter Review

Practice writing these letters on the lines below. You have mastered the letters M, m, N, n, O, o. Congratulations!

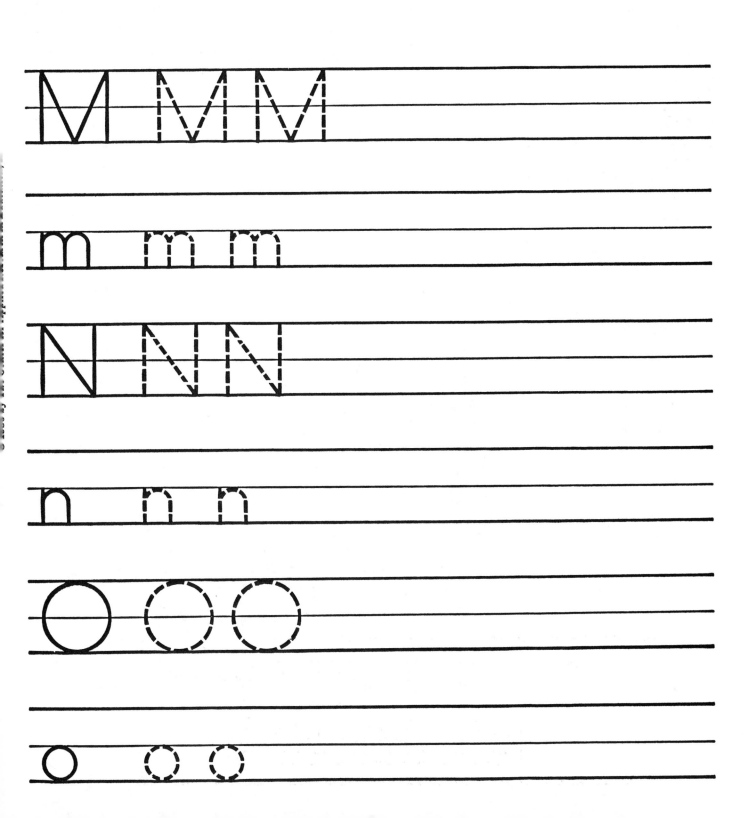

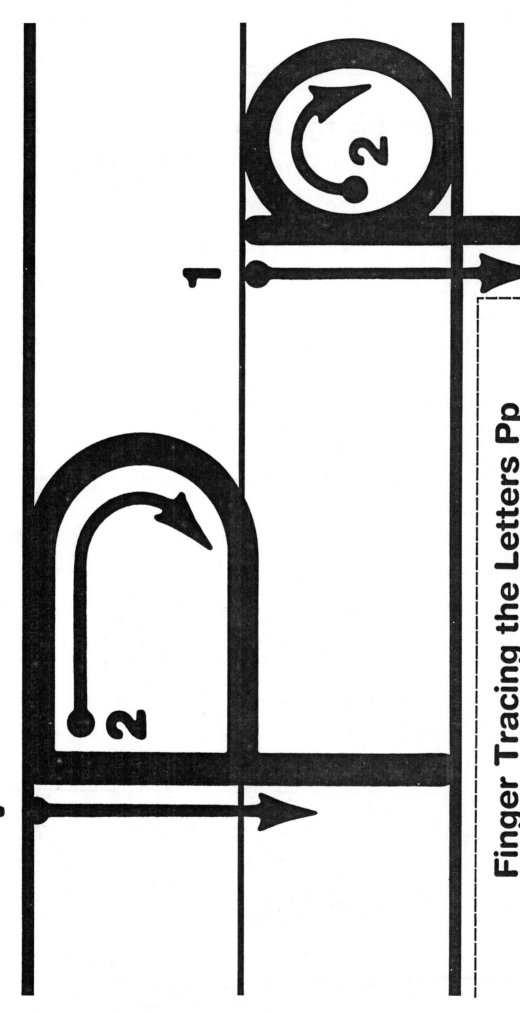

Finger Tracing the Letters Pp

Reproduce this page for each child in your class. Have each child cut along the dotted line and discard the teacher directions. Then help each one glue popped popcorn or dried peas on the heavy black lines using white glue and making sure not to cover up the direction arrows.

When the glue is dry, have each child trace over the letters using the first finger and following the directions indicated by the numbered arrows.

Place the finished letter sheet with the child's name on the back in a shoebox for each child and locate the boxes in a convenient place where the children can practice tracing the letters daily. This will help them remember the names of the letters and the correct way to form them.

Name _____

Pirate Pete

Pirate Pete is really a pest! He pursues people all over the Pacific in his sailing ship, the Pink Parrot. Pieces of gold are his prize. Here is Pirate Pete under a palm tree. Color all of the things that begin with the sound of **p** in this picture.

Name _____

Pirate Pete's Prize

Pirate Pete has found a treasure chest full of gold, but not all of the gold is real. If the coin has a picture of something that starts with the sound of **p**, it's real gold. Find the 8 pieces of real gold on this page, cut them out, and glue them inside the treasure chest. Then draw your own **p** picture coin. Glue gold glitter on the coins.

Name _____

Pirate Pete's Patches

Pirate Pete really gets tired of wearing the same old eye patch all the time. He'd like you to create some perky new patches for him. Here's what you do:

1. Color or draw on the patches below in any way you like.
2. Cut out the patches.
3. Cover the back of each hole with tape to reinforce it.
4. Use a hole puncher to punch out the holes.
5. Tie a piece of string or sewing elastic to each hole. Then tie the patch to fit your head.

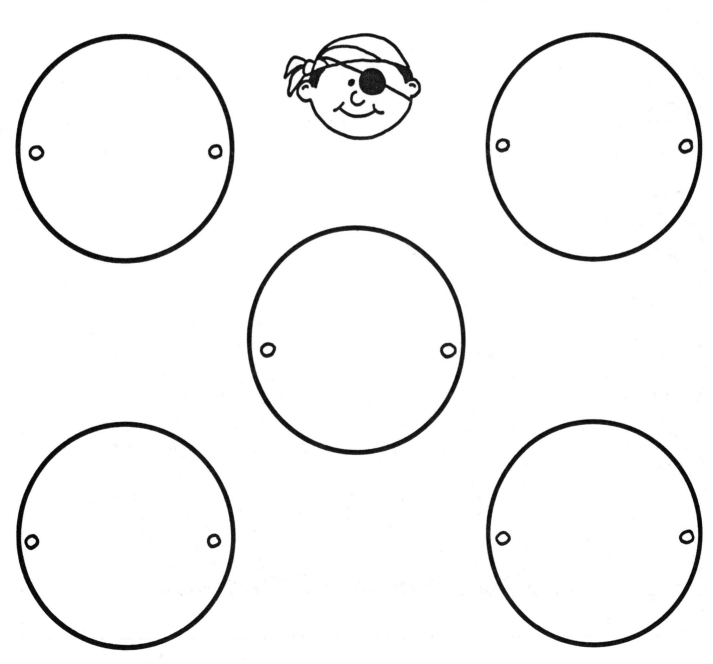

Name _____

P p Puzzle

To solve this puzzle, color the capital **P** spaces yellow. What **p** picture did you find?

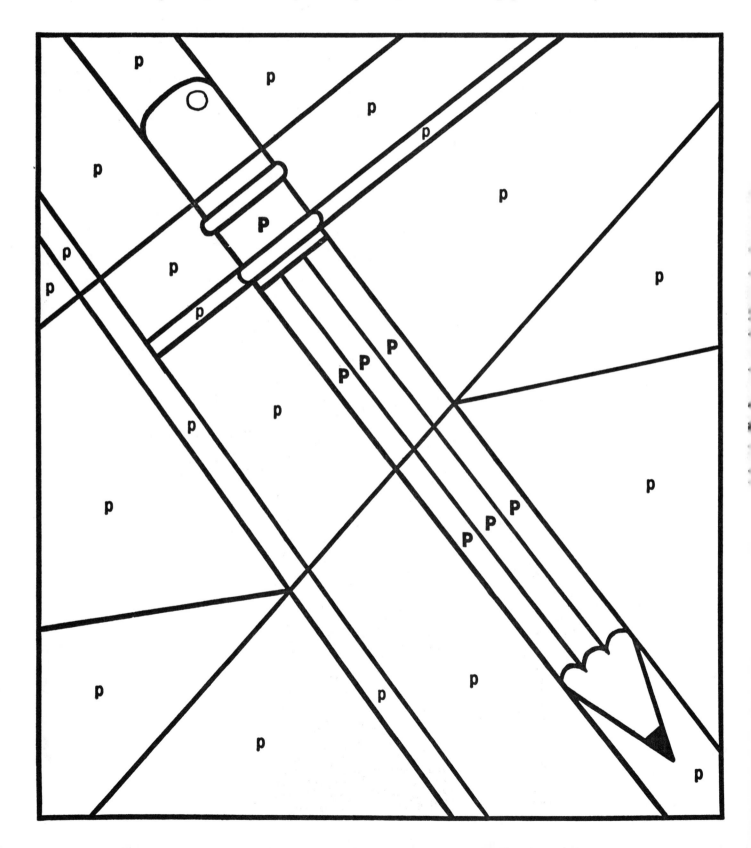

Name _____

Pirate Pete's Popsicles
(Serves 6–8)

You need:

4 cups apple juice
1 8-ounce carton plain or vanilla
  yogurt
1 apple (cut in tiny pieces)

Directions:
Place all of the ingredients into a blender and blend until smooth. Pour the mixture into popsicle molds, small paper cups, or ice tray sections. Make sure to put in a popsicle stick for each pop. Place in the freezer until firm.

Finger Tracing the Letters Q q

Reproduce this page for each child in your class. Have each child cut along the dotted line and discard the teacher directions. Then help each child glue one glue quilt pieces (fabric scraps) on the heavy black lines using white glue and making sure not to cover up the direction arrows.

When the glue is dry, have each child trace over the letters using the first finger and following the directions indicated by the numbered arrows.

Place the finished letter sheet with the child's name on the back in a shoebox for each child and locate the boxes in a convenient place where the children can practice tracing the letters daily. This will help them remember the names of the letters and the correct way to form them.

Name _____

Queen Quinella

Queen Quinella is quietly making a quilt. Her duck Quincy is quacking his approval. Will Queen Quinella finish the quilt as a surprise for the King's birthday? Help her by coloring the quilt pieces with as many different colors and designs as you can.

Name _____

Find Quincy Game (For 2 players)

To help the Queen find Quincy here's what you do:

1. The first player places a marker on Bridge 1. She moves ahead on each steppingstone if she can give a word beginning with the letter on the stone. She must stop if she makes a mistake or reaches the next bridge.
2. The next player takes his turn in the same way.
3. The first player to reach Quincy wins.

Name _____

Quincy's Hidden Objects

Quincy has hidden 5 objects in the woods near the castle Find each one and color it any color you would like.

Answers: bird, bone, apple, necklace, ring

Name _____

Queen Quinella's Q Game
(For 2 players)

To play Queen Quinella's Q game, follow these directions:

1. Glue the Q gameboard to a piece of heavy construction paper.
2. Place the gameboard on a smooth floor.
3. The first player stands directly over the gameboard and drops a penny from waist height. If the penny lands in a space, the player names the **q** picture and gets the point in the circle in that space if he or she is correct. Then the second player takes a turn.
4. If the penny lands on a line or off the gameboard, the player takes turns until it lands in a **q** space. The first player to earn 10 points wins!

Name _____

Q q Puzzle

To solve this puzzle, color the lower-case **q** spaces yellow. Color the capital **Q** spaces any color you would like. What **q** sound does the animal in this picture make?

Name _____

Queen Quinella's Quiche (Serves 8)

You need:

1 pound sausage (sliced)
1 small onion (chopped)
1 9″ uncooked deep-dish pie shell
6 eggs

Directions:
Brown the sausage and onion together in a non-stick frying pan. Drain off the excess grease **(use caution).** Spread the sausage and onion mixture on the bottom of the pie shell. Beat the eggs with a fork in a small bowl and pour them over the sausage and onion mixture. Bake in a 350° oven for 50 minutes.

Finger Tracing the Letters R r

Reproduce this page for each child in your class. Have each child cut along the dotted line and discard the teacher directions. Then help each child glue one glue ribbons or uncooked rice on the heavy black lines using white glue and making sure not to cover up the direction arrows.

When the glue is dry, have each child trace over the letters using the first finger and following the directions indicated by the numbered arrows.

Place the finished letter sheet with the child's name on the back in a shoebox for each child and locate the boxes in a convenient place where the children can practice tracing the letters daily. This will help them remember the names of the letters and the correct way to form them.

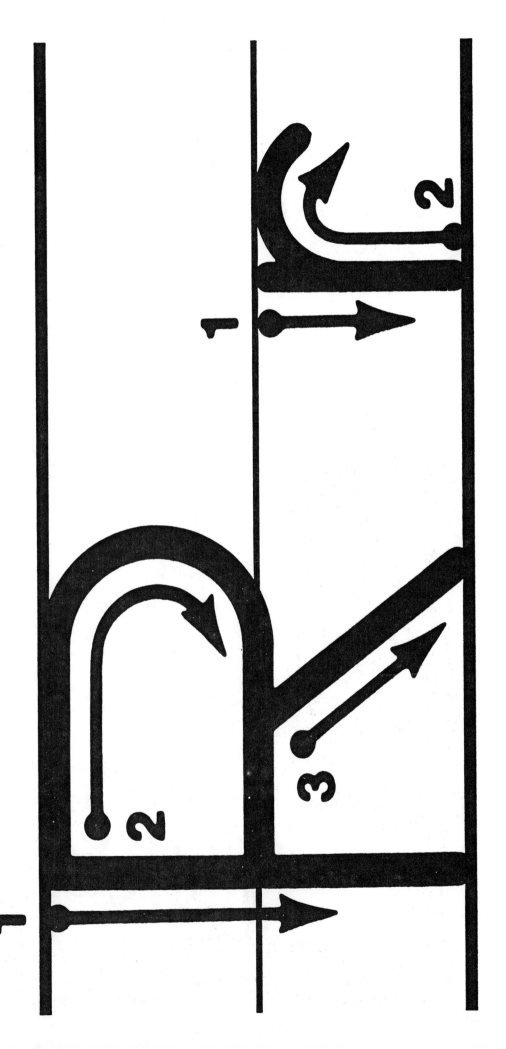

Name _____

Randy Reindeer

Randy the reindeer lives in Rhode Island. His friend Ranger Robert is a real rascal! Sometimes he feeds Randy raspberries. The raspberries give Randy a terrible red rash. Color Ranger Robert and Randy, and color Randy's spots red.

Name _____

Make Randy with Shapes

To help Randy recover from his rash, here's what you do:

1. Color the pieces on this page and on page Rr-3.
2. Cut them out.
3. Glue Randy's face together as shown in this picture.

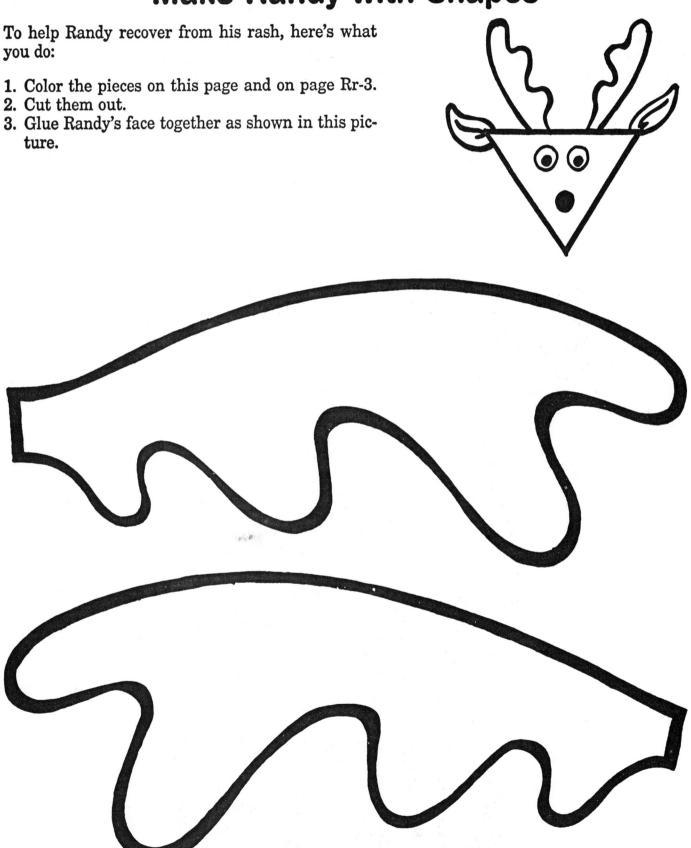

Name _____

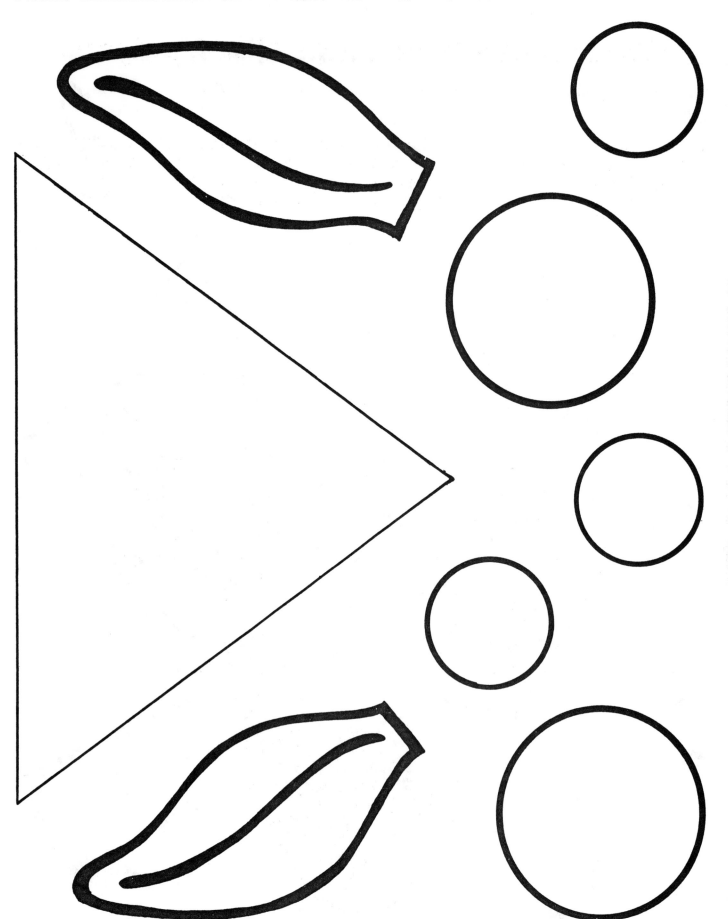

Name _____

Randy's Reindeer Game (For 2 players)

To play Randy's reindeer game, here's what you do:

1. Place a marker for each player on the capital R.
2. The player wearing the most red clothing goes first. He tosses a penny in the air. If it lands face up, he moves ahead 2 spaces. If it lands face down, he moves ahead 1 space. The player must name the **r** picture in the space he lands on.
3. The second player takes a turn in the same way. The first player to return to the letter R is the winner.

Name _____

R r Puzzle

To solve this puzzle, color the lower-case **r** spaces light brown. Color the capital **R** spaces any color you would like. What **r** picture did you find?

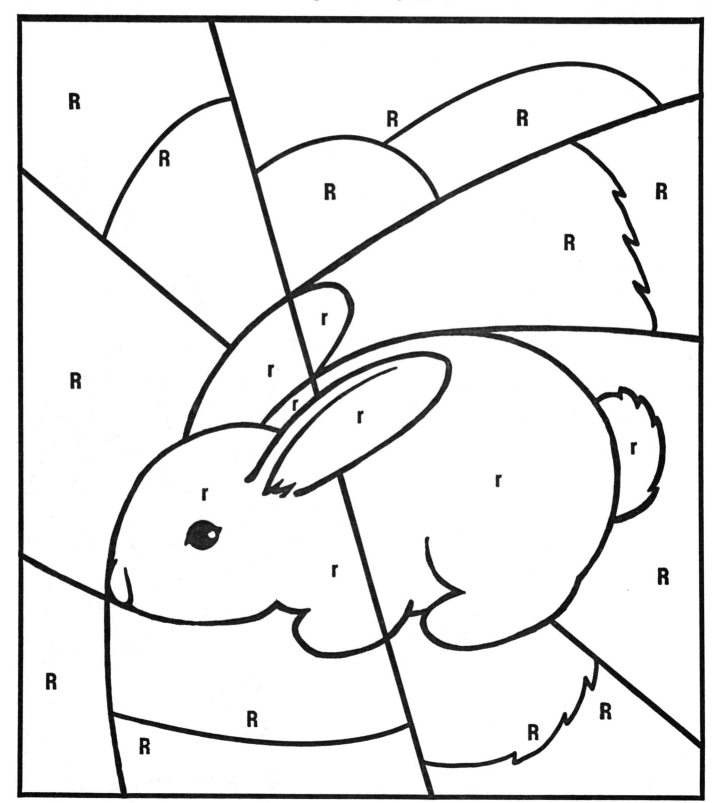

Name _____

Randy's Rice Pudding (Serves 6)

You need:

2 cups white rice (cooked)
1⅓ cups milk
4 tablespoons honey
1½ tablespoons soft butter
1 teaspoon vanilla
3 eggs (well beaten)
⅓ cup raisins (presoaked in water)
1 teaspoon lemon juice
1 cup granola cereal

Directions:
Prepare the cooked rice and set aside. Combine the milk, honey, butter, vanilla, and eggs in a large bowl with a wooden spoon. Add the raisins and lemon juice. Stir the cooked rice into the liquid mixture and combine well. Grease a 2- to 3-quart baking dish with butter. Sprinkle the bottom evenly with ½ cup of the granola cereal. Spread the rice mixture evenly over the cereal and cover it with the remaining granola. Bake the rice pudding in a 325° oven for 50 minutes. Enjoy it while it's warm!

Name _____

P Q R Letter Review

Practice writing these letters on the lines below. You have mastered the letters P, p, Q, q, R, r. Congratulations!

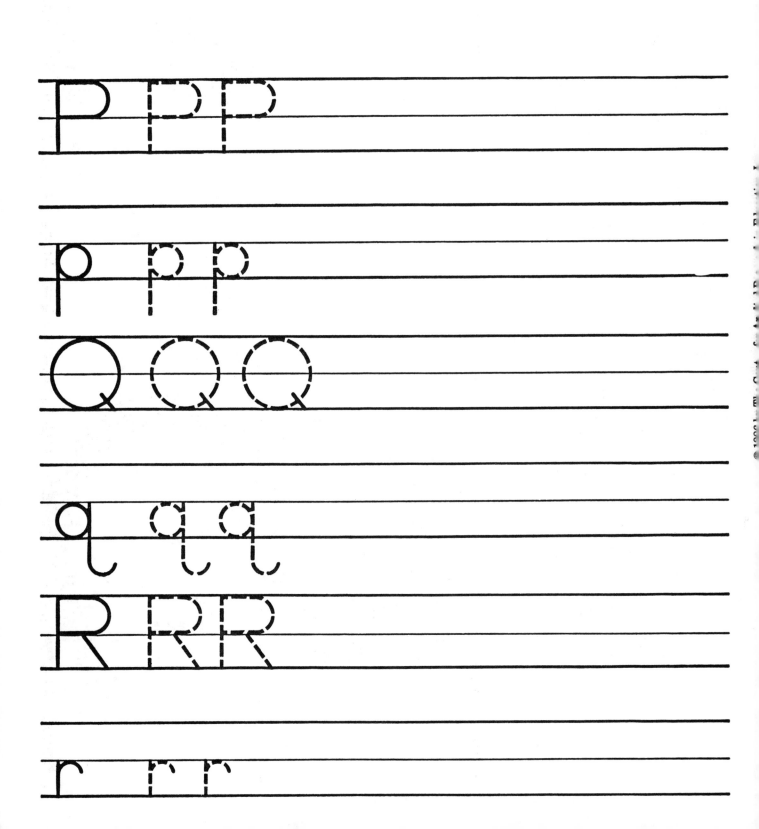

Finger Tracing the Letters S s

Reproduce this page for each child in your class. Have each child cut along the dotted line and discard the teacher directions. Then help each one glue sunflower seeds on the heavy black lines using white glue and making sure not to cover up the direction arrows.

When the glue is dry, have each child trace over the letters using the first finger and following the directions indicated by the numbered arrows.

Place the finished letter sheet with the child's name on the back in a shoebox for each child and locate the boxes in a convenient place where the children can practice tracing the letters daily. This will help them remember the names of the letters and the correct way to form them.

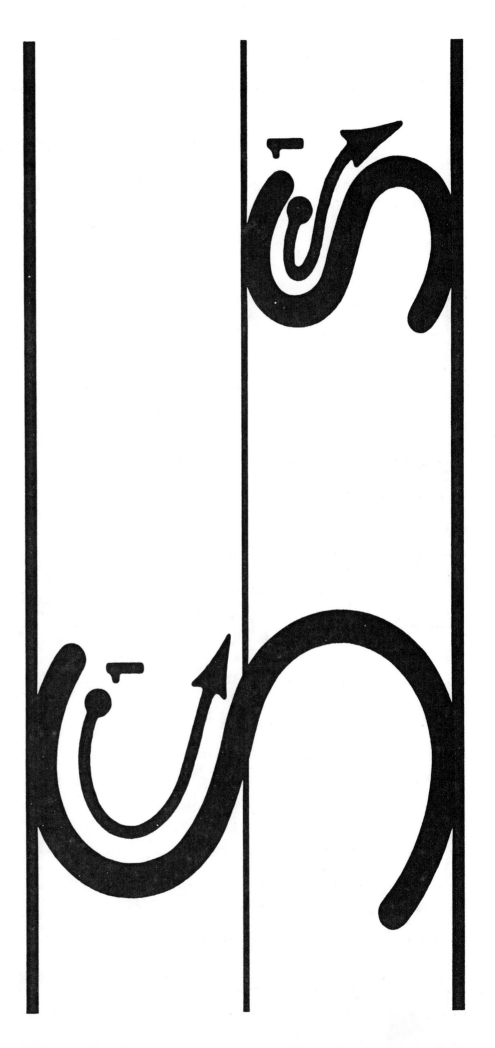

Name _____

Sammy Snowman

Sammy the snowman thinks snow is sensational! He spends his favorite season (can you guess which one?) in South Dakota. Help Sammy spruce up his outfit by coloring his scarf scarlet. Then color the rest of the picture if you like.

Name _____

Find Homes for Sammy's Friends

Sammy Snowman has many forest friends. They like to stop by and visit him, but when the snow starts falling they scurry to their homes. Help Sammy's friends find their homes. Color each animal, cut it out, and glue it to its home. Then color the rest of the picture.

Name _____

Make Sammy Snowman

To make Sammy Snowman, here's what you do:

1. Glue a large ball of newspaper to the center of a white paper plate using white glue.
2. Glue a smaller ball of newspaper on top of the larger ball. Let dry.
3. Pour ½ cup warm water into a large bowl and add 2 cups of Ivory Snow. Let this mixture stand for 2 minutes. Then use an electric mixer (**caution**) or hand beater to whip the soap until frothy. Gradually add ½ cup more warm water until the soap stands in peaks.
4. Scoop the soap mixture with your hand and completely cover the newspaper balls to make a snowman. Pat it gently to press the soap to the newspaper.
5. Make Sammy's face with small stones or beads. Use 2 small twigs for his arms and make a hat and scarf with construction paper.
6. Let Sammy dry overnight.

Name _____

Sammy's S Game (For 2 players)

To play Sammy's S game, follow these directions:

1. Glue the S gameboard to a sheet of heavy construction paper.
2. Place the gameboard on a smooth floor.
3. The first player stands directly over the gameboard and drops a penny from waist height. If the penny lands in a space, the player names the **s** picture and gets the point in the circle in that space if he or she is correct. Then the second player takes a turn.
4. If the penny lands on a line or off the gameboard, the player takes turns until it lands in an **s** space. The first player to earn 10 points wins!

Name _____

S s Puzzle

To solve this puzzle, color the capital **S** spaces any color you would like. What **s** picture did you find?

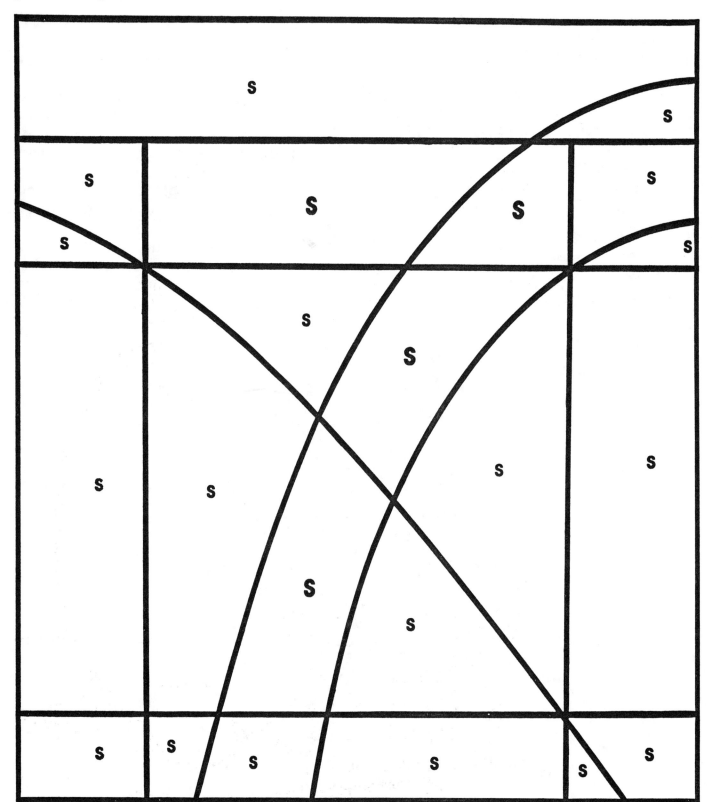

Name _____

Sammy's Snowball Dessert (Serves 1)

You need:

vanilla ice cream or frozen yogurt
shredded coconut
maraschino cherries

Directions:
1. Use an ice cream scoop to make a round ball of ice cream or frozen yogurt.
2. Place the ball on a piece of waxed paper and cover with shredded coconut. Gently roll the ball to cover it.
3. Push a few maraschino cherries into it for decoration.
4. Place the snowball in a plastic bag and freeze until solid.

Finger Tracing the Letters T t

Reproduce this page for each child in your class. Have each child cut along the dotted line and discard the teacher directions. Then help each one glue toothpicks on the heavy black lines using white glue and making sure not to cover up the direction arrows.

When the glue is dry, have each child trace over the letters using the first finger and following the directions indicated by the numbered arrows.

Place the finished letter sheet with the child's name on the back in a shoebox for each child and locate the boxes in a convenient place where the children can practice tracing the letters daily. This will help them remember the names of the letters and the correct way to form them.

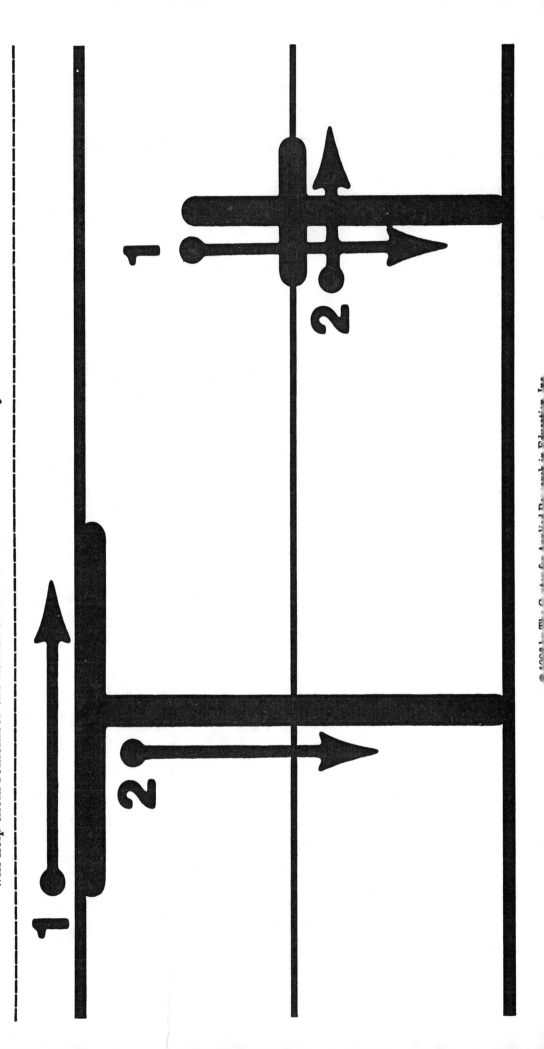

Name _____

Tillie Tortoise

Tillie the tortoise is traveling to Texas by way of the Timberline Trail. She often gets tired and stops for a rest. While she is resting, help Tillie find 9 things in this picture that begin with the t sound. Color each t picture any color you would like.

ANSWERS: trees, truck, tires, tricycle, tent, table, turtle (Timothy), tadpole, trail

Name _____

Make Tillie Tortoise

To make Tillie Tortoise, here's what you do:

1. Cut out about 65 1″ green tissue paper squares.
2. Turn a 16-ounce cottage cheese container upside down and rub liquid starch or white glue all over the outside.
3. Glue the tissue paper squares to cover the outside. Let dry for several hours.
4. Color the tortoise body on this page and cut it out.
5. Glue the cottage cheese container to the dotted lines with white glue.

Name _____

Tillie's T Game (For 2 players)

During Tillie's travels on the Timberline Trail she saw many interesting things that begin with the **t** sound. To find out what they were, here's what you do:

1. Glue this page to a sheet of heavy construction paper, let dry, and cut out.
2. Cut a piece of string 11″ long.
3. Use a hole puncher to punch the holes at the top and bottom of the trail.
4. Thread the string through the hole at the top of the trail and tape the end to the back of the sheet.
5. String a large button (green if you can find one) onto the trail string.
6. Place the free end of the string through the hole at the bottom of the trail and tape the end to the back.
7. Move Tillie (the button) along the trail and name each **t** picture she passes.

Name _____

T t Puzzle

To solve this puzzle, color the lower-case **t** spaces tan. Color the capital **T** spaces any color you like. What **t** picture did you find?

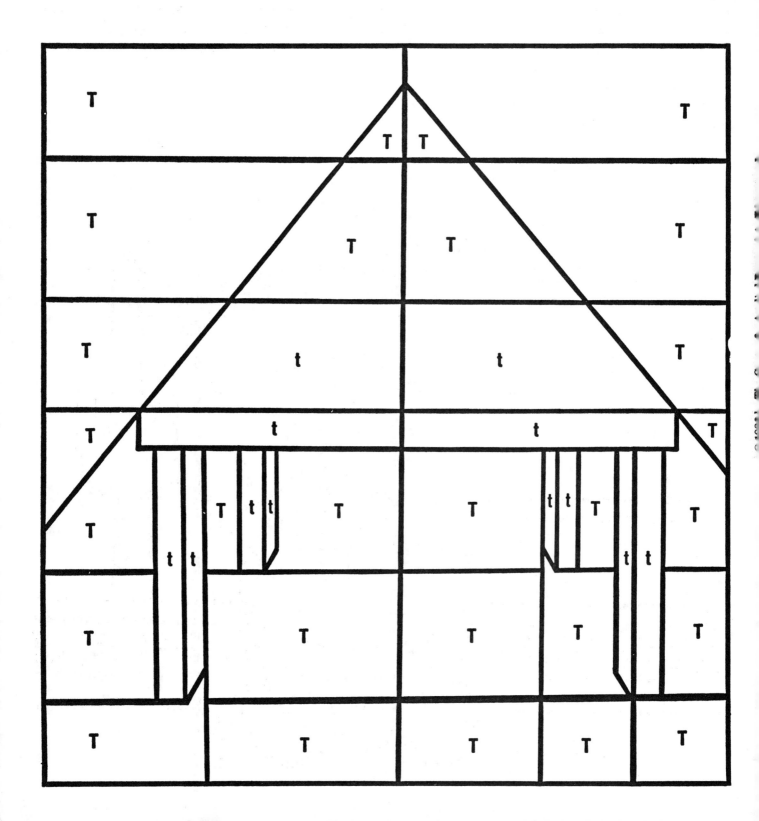

Name _____

Tillie's Texas Tacos (Serves 6)

You need:

1 pound ground meat
1 cup grated yellow cheese (mild cheddar or colby)
1 cup chopped tomatoes
½ cup chopped black olives
1 cup shredded lettuce
1 package prepared taco shells
mild taco sauce (*optional*)

Directions:
Brown ground meat in a skillet. Drain off the fat. Place the cooked hamburger, grated cheese, chopped olives, chopped tomatoes, and shredded lettuce into separate serving bowls. Now put your favorite ingredients into your taco shell and enjoy!

Finger Tracing the Letters U u

Reproduce this page for each child in your class. Have each child cut along the dotted line and discard the teacher directions. Then help each child one glue one glue u-shaped macaroni elbows on the heavy black lines using white glue and making sure not to cover up the direction arrows.

When the glue is dry, have each child trace over the letters using the first finger and following the directions indicated by the numbered arrows.

Place the finished letter sheet with the child's name on the back in a shoebox for each child and locate the boxes in a convenient place where the children can practice tracing the letters daily. This will help them remember the names of the letters and the correct way to form them.

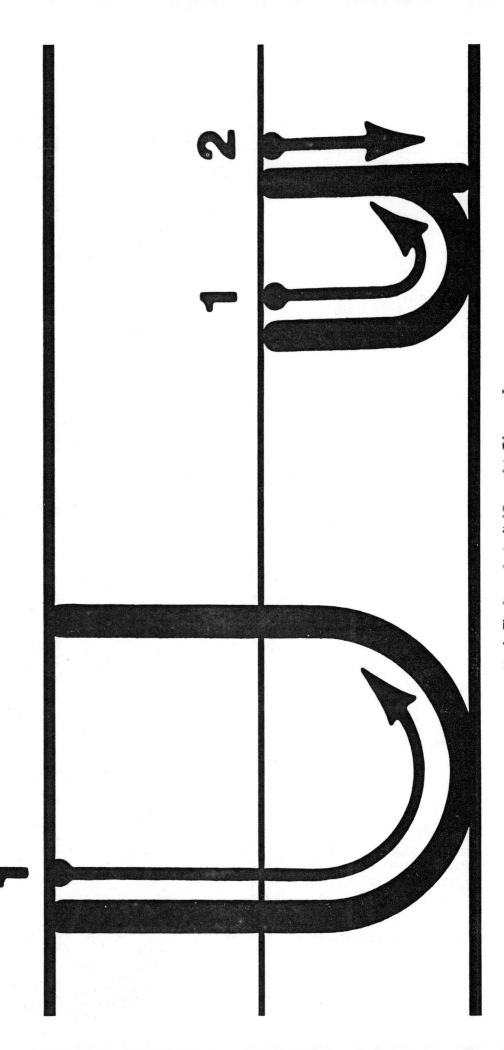

Name _____

Ubie Unicorn

Ubie the unicorn loves to play his ukulele while riding his unicycle. He performs for the Uptown Amusement Park in Utah and must wear a uniform to work. Help Ubie get ready to go to work by coloring his uniform for him. Use some unusual colors!

Name _____

Make Your Own Ukulele

To make your own ukulele to play along with Ubie, here's what you do:

1. Attach the center of a 9″ pie tin to a sanded strip of wood 18″ × 1″ × ¼″. Use a short nail or thumbtack and attach it a few inches from the end of the wood strip. (Hammer the nail flat on the back side.)
2. Use a tin snips (**caution**) to make four ½″ cuts about ½″ apart on opposite sides of the pie tin (eight cuts in all).
3. Brush the cut edges of the pie pan with white glue and let dry. This will cover rough edges.
4. Get 4 rubber bands of various widths and stretch each one from one cut side of the pie tin to its matching cut on the opposite side.
5. Now play your ukulele along with your favorite record! Ubie's uncle in Utah taught him how to play.

Name _____

Ubie's U Game (For 2 players)

You can play this thinking game with a friend. Here's what you do:

1. Glue the card sheet below onto a piece of heavy paper and let dry.
2. Cut out the cards, shuffle them, and spread them on a table face down.
3. The first player turns 2 cards face up to try to make a pair. If the cards match, he keeps them and the second player takes a turn. If they do not match, he turns them face down and the second player looks for a pair. The player with the most pairs of **u** cards wins.

Name _____

U u Puzzle

To solve this puzzle, color the capital **U** spaces brown. What **u** picture did you find?

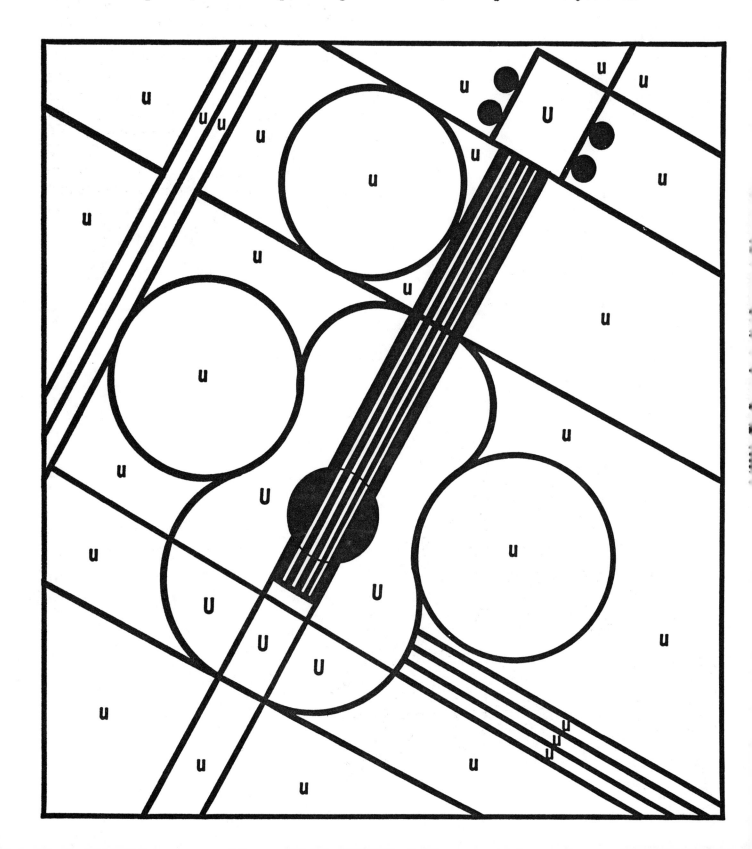

Name _____

Ubie's Upside-Down Cake (Serves 8)

You need:

½ cup butter
1 cup brown sugar (firmly packed)
1 2½-ounce package pecan halves
1 5¼-ounce can pineapple slices
1 4-ounce jar maraschino cherries
1 yellow cake mix (with ingredients)

Directions:
Melt the butter in a skillet and add the brown sugar. Stir with a wooden spoon until dissolved. Pour the sugar mixture into 1 of 2 cake pans. Sprinkle pecans into the cake pan. Drain the juice from the pineapple. Place a maraschino cherry in the center of each pineapple slice in the bottom of the cake pan. Prepare the cake batter following the package directions. Pour the cake batter over the ingredients in the cake pan. Pour the remaining cake batter into the second cake pan. Bake according to the package directions. When cool, turn out the plain cake onto a plate with the other cake on top.

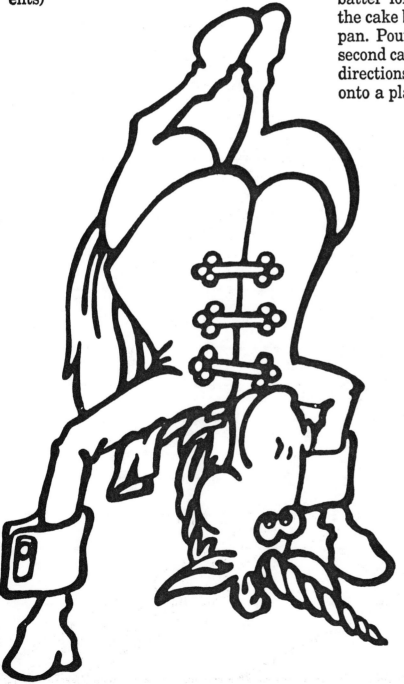

Name _____

S T U Letter Review

Practice writing these letters on the lines below. You have mastered the letters S, s, T, t, U, u. Congratulations!

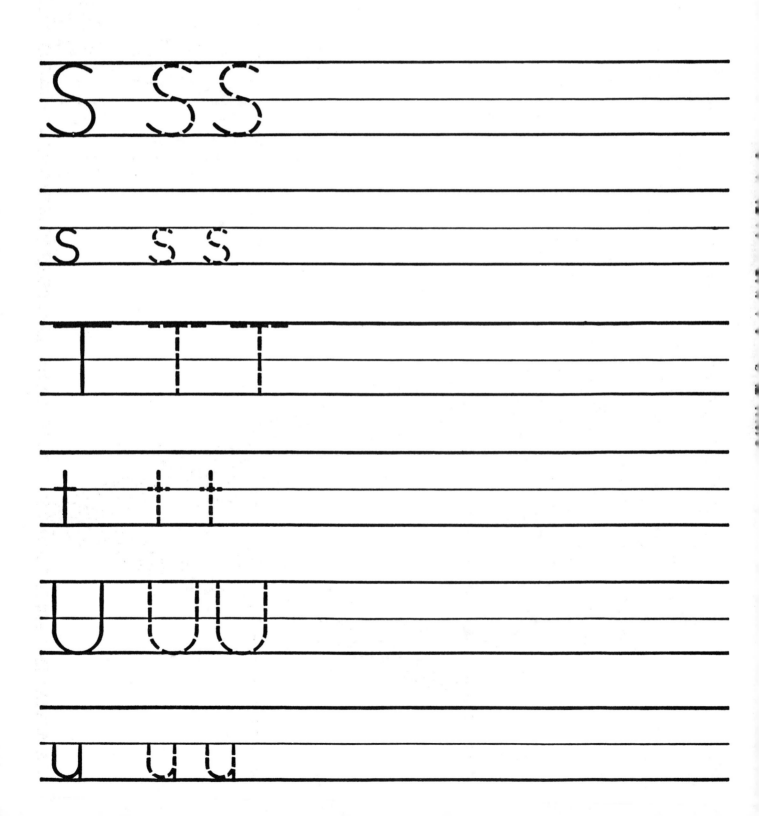

Finger Tracing the Letters V v

Reproduce this page for each child in your class. Have each child cut along the dotted line and discard the teacher directions. Then help each child glue one glue purple "violets" (little pieces of tissue paper curled around the end of a pencil) on the heavy black lines using white glue and making sure not to cover up the direction arrows.

When the glue is dry, have each child trace over the letters using the first finger and following the directions indicated by the numbered arrows.

Place the finished letter sheet with the child's name on the back in a shoebox for each child and locate the boxes in a convenient place where the children can practice tracing the letters daily. This will help them remember the names of the letters and the correct way to form them.

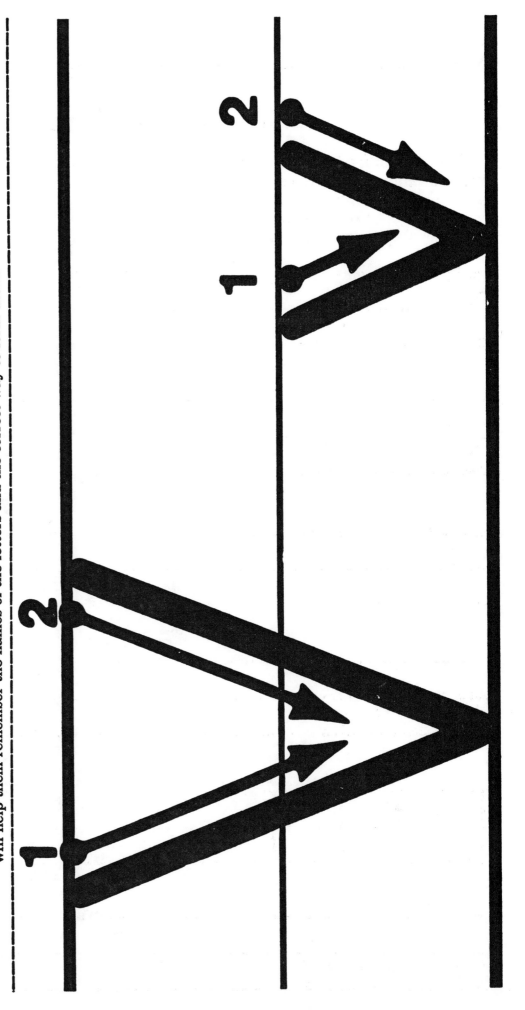

Name _____

Vinnie Vulture

Vinnie the vulture is viewing the valley from his vantage point in Vermont. He's a real flashy dresser, and loves to wear brightly colored vests. Color Vinnie's vest violet, then color the rest of the picture.

Name _____

Make Vests for Vinnie

To make more vests for Vinnie, here's what you do:

1. Color the vests below in a variety of ways. Remember, he likes them very flashy!
2. Cut out the vests and the picture of Vinnie on page Vv-1. Then try on the vests and use the tabs to keep them in place.

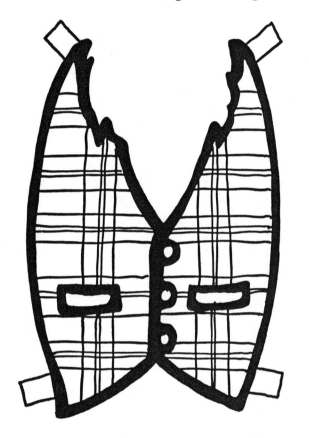

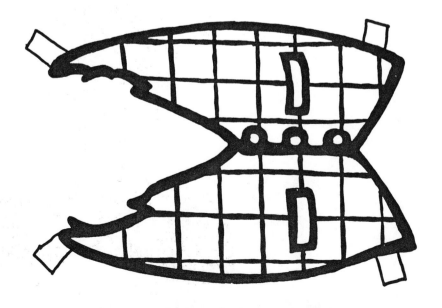

Name _____

Vinnie's Visor

Vinnie and his friends wear their visors when they're viewing the valley. To make a visor like Vinnie's, here's what you do:

1. Color the visor below and cut it out. Decorate it with glitter, stickers, tissue paper, dried flowers, or anything else you can attach with white glue.
2. Cut a piece of 1″ wide ribbon or construction paper to fit your head with about 6″ extra.
3. Staple the visor in the center of the ribbon or paper strip. Make sure the top of the visor is against the top of the ribbon or paper strip edge.
4. Tie on the visor (or staple it if you used a paper strip). Now you can do your own viewing!

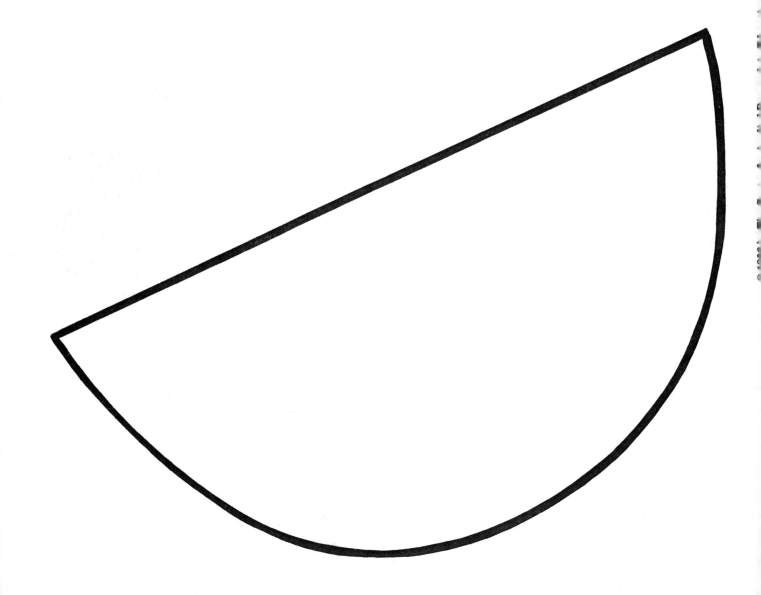

Name _____

Match Vinnie's Valentines

Vinnie is a very popular vulture. He has many friends and enjoys doing nice things for them. He wanted to buy 2 matching valentine cards for 2 of his friends and surprise them on Valentine's Day. Help Vinnie find 2 valentines on this page that are exactly the same. Then cut them out and glue them into Vinnie's wings.

Name _____

Vinnie's V Game (For 2 players)

To play Vinnie's V game, here's what you do:

1. Place a marker for each player on the capital **V.**
2. The player wearing the most violet clothing goes first. He or she tosses a penny in the air. If it lands face up, he moves ahead 2 spaces. If it lands face down, he moves ahead 1 space. The player must name the **v** picture in the space he lands on.
3. The second player takes a turn in the same way. The first player to reach the lower-case **v** is the winner.

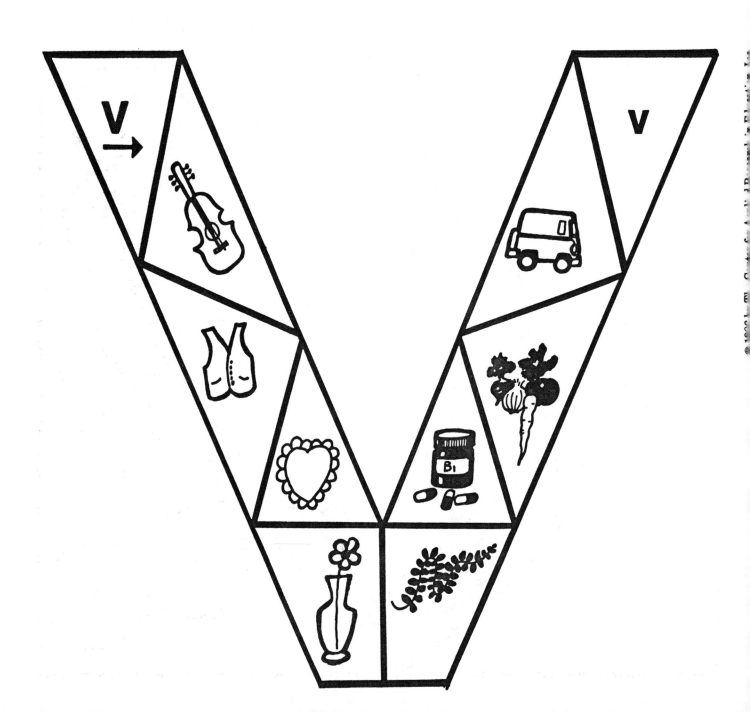

Name _____

V v Puzzle

To solve this puzzle, color the lower-case **v** spaces either red, pink, or violet. What **v** picture did you find?

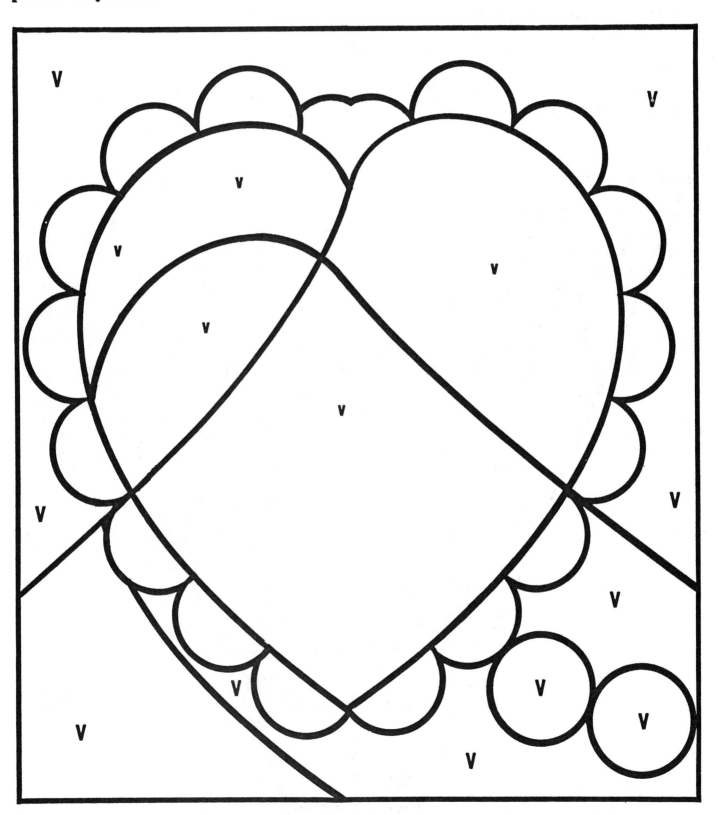

Name _____

Vinnie's Vegetable Soup (Serves 4–6)

You need:

2 tablespoons butter
½ cup diced onions
1 cup diced carrots
½ cup diced celery
1 cup canned tomatoes
3 large potatoes (sliced)
1 can corn
6 cups water or soup stock
seasonings to taste

Directions:
In a skillet brown the onions in the butter. Place the browned onions and the remaining ingredients into a large pot. (You can add to or substitute for any of the vegetables if you like.) Cover and simmer the soup over low heat for 45 minutes. Add your own seasonings to taste.

Finger Tracing the Letters W w

Reproduce this page for each child in your class. Have each child cut along the dotted line and discard the teacher directions. Then help each one glue watermelon seeds on the heavy black lines using white glue and making sure not to cover up the direction arrows.

When the glue is dry, have each child trace over the letters using the first finger and following the directions indicated by the numbered arrows.

Place the finished letter sheet with the child's name on the back in a shoebox for each child and locate the boxes in a convenient place where the children can practice tracing the letters daily. This will help them remember the names of the letters and the correct way to form them.

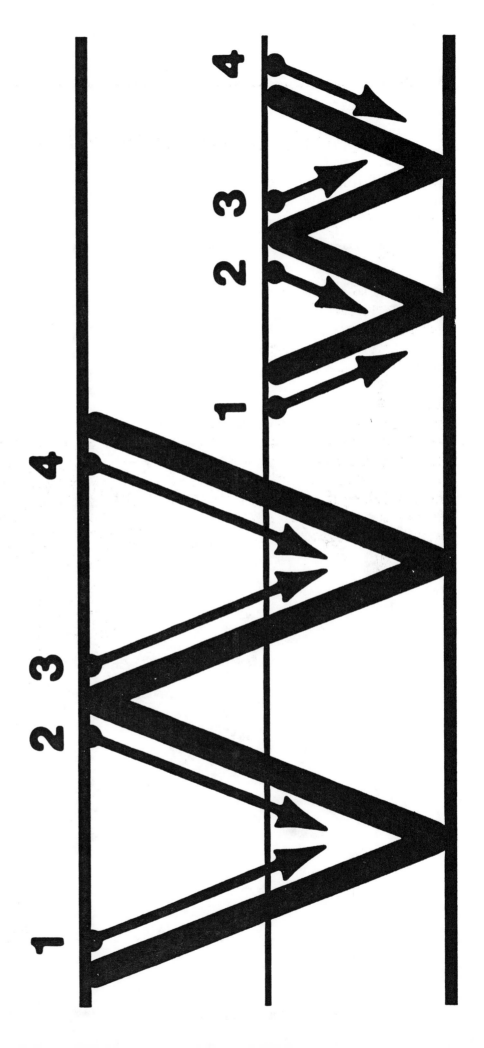

Name _____

Wild Willie

Wild Willie is wanted in the West for winking at women. He was last seen in a covered wagon in Wisconsin. Help the sheriff find Wild Willie by completing his face on this wanted poster.

Name _____

Wagon Wheel Art

Wild Willie thinks wheels are wonderful! He decorates his wagon with them. To make your own wheel art for your wall, here's what you do:

1. In each wheel section draw designs as in the sample below. Try using different shapes such as stars, squares, lightning bolts, rainbows, etc.
2. Color in each wheel section using only one color.
3. Cut out the wheels and tape them to your wall!

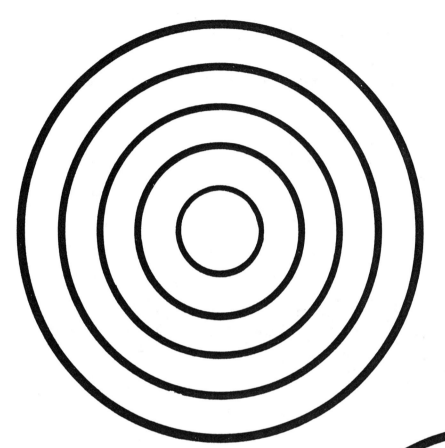

Name _____

Match the Wagons

While Wild Willie was wandering through Wisconsin, he witnessed a wonderful sight! He saw two kinds of wagons winding their way West. He suggested to the wagon master that these wagons form wagon trains. Help the wagon master arrange these wagons into two wagon trains so that all of the wagons in each train are alike in some way. Cut out the wagons on this page and glue them to the trails on page Ww-4.

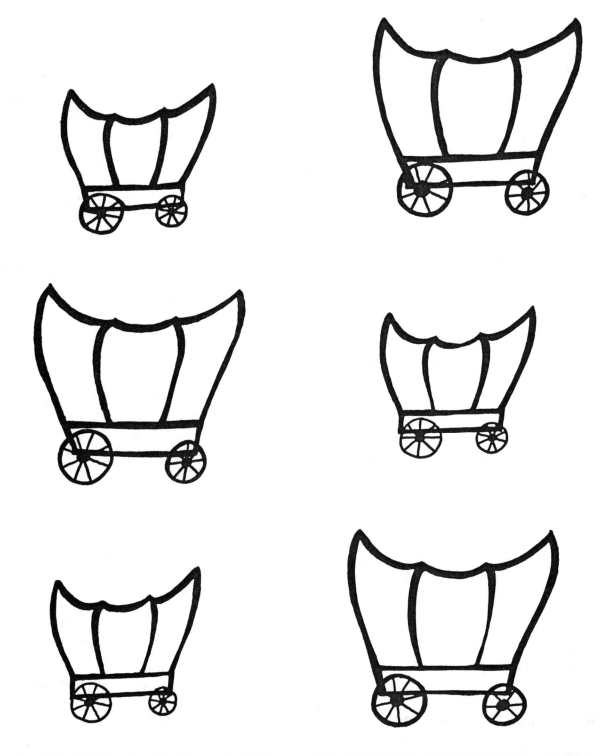

Name _____

Name _____

Wagons West Game (For 4 players)

To make and play the Wagons West game, here's what you do:

1. Color each wagon on this page a different color.
2. Cut out the wagon markers. Cut a slit at the end of each marker on the line, fold the marker on the solid lines, then interlock the slits so the marker stands up.
3. To play the game, use the gameboard on page Ww-6 and have each player place a marker on the capital **W**.
4. The player wearing the most white clothing goes first. He or she tosses a penny in the air. If it lands face up, he moves ahead 2 spaces. If it lands face down, he moves ahead 1 space. The player must name the **w** picture in the space he lands on or follow the directions in the space.
5. The next player wearing the most white goes second in the same way, and the rest of the players do the same. The first player to reach the lower-case **w** is the winner.

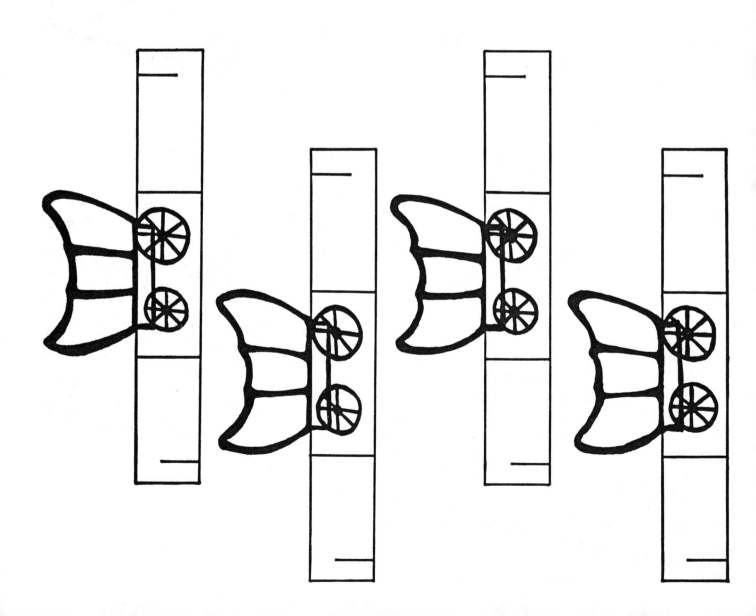

Name _____

A wolf walks in front of your wagon. Go back 3 spaces.

Go ahead 1 space.

Go back 1 space.

Go ahead 2 spaces.

Name _____

W w Puzzle

To solve this puzzle, color the capital W spaces yellow. Color the lower-case **w** spaces red. What **w** picture did you find?

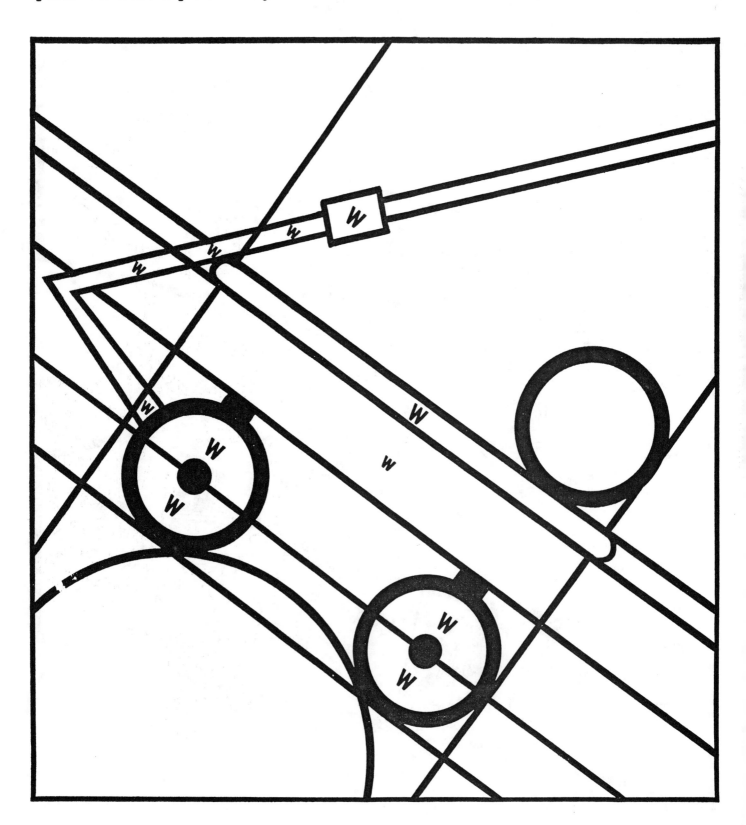

Name _____

Wild Willie's Wonderful Waffles (Serves 4)

You need:

1¾ cups whole-wheat flour
2 teaspoons double-acting baking soda
3 eggs (separated)
2 teaspoons honey
3 teaspoons melted butter
1½ cups milk
your favorite syrup or toppings

Directions:
Sift the flour and baking soda together. Carefully separate the egg yolks from the egg whites. Combine the flour mixture with the egg yolks, honey, butter, and milk in a small bowl. In a separate small bowl beat the 3 egg whites with a fork until stiff but not dry. Using a wooden spoon, carefully fold them into the batter. Pour some batter into the waffle iron and cook until done. Enjoy with your favorite syrup or toppings!

Finger Tracing the Letters X x

Reproduce this page for each child in your class. Have each child cut along the dotted line and discard the teacher directions. Then help each one glue rolled x's of aluminum foil on the heavy black lines using white glue and making sure not to cover up the direction arrows.

When the glue is dry, have each child trace over the letters using the first finger and following the directions indicated by the numbered arrows.

Place the finished letter sheet with the child's name on the back in a shoebox for each child and locate the boxes in a convenient place where the children can practice tracing the letters daily. This will help them remember the names of the letters and the correct way to form them.

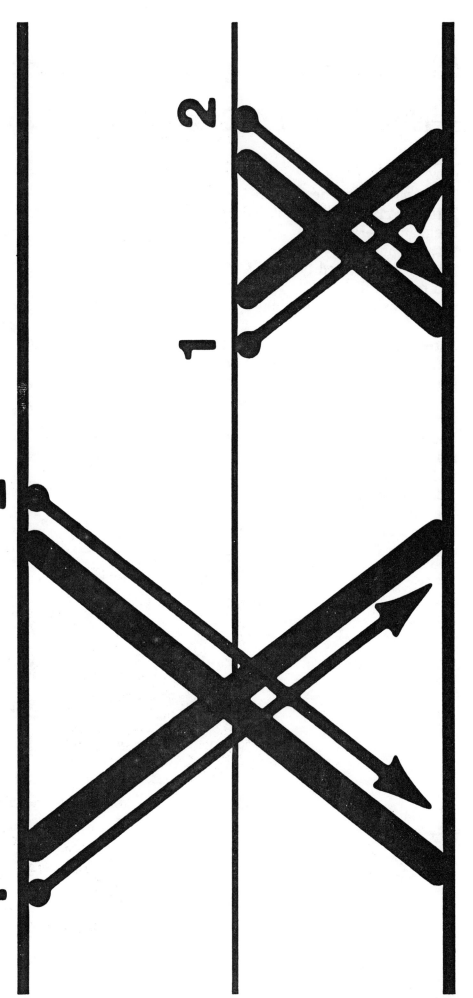

Name _____

X-Caliber from X-Eron

X-Caliber is from the planet X-Eron. He has X-ray eyes that allow him to see things we can't. He is in excellent health because he exercises every day. He would be extra excited if you would color his spacesuit for him.

Name _____

X-Caliber's Unusual Home

X-Caliber's home on the planet X-Eron is very unusual! This is a picture of his kitchen. Color each of the unusual things you see in this kitchen, and think of a way X-Caliber would use each item.

Name _____

X-Caliber's X Collage

As you might guess, X-Caliber's favorite letter is **x**. On his planet, X-Eron, many words begin with the letter **x**. Here on earth the letter **x** is found mostly in the middle or at the ends of words. Help X-Caliber learn about earth's **x** words. Collect magazine pictures or words that contain the letter **x** and glue them on the letter **X** below.

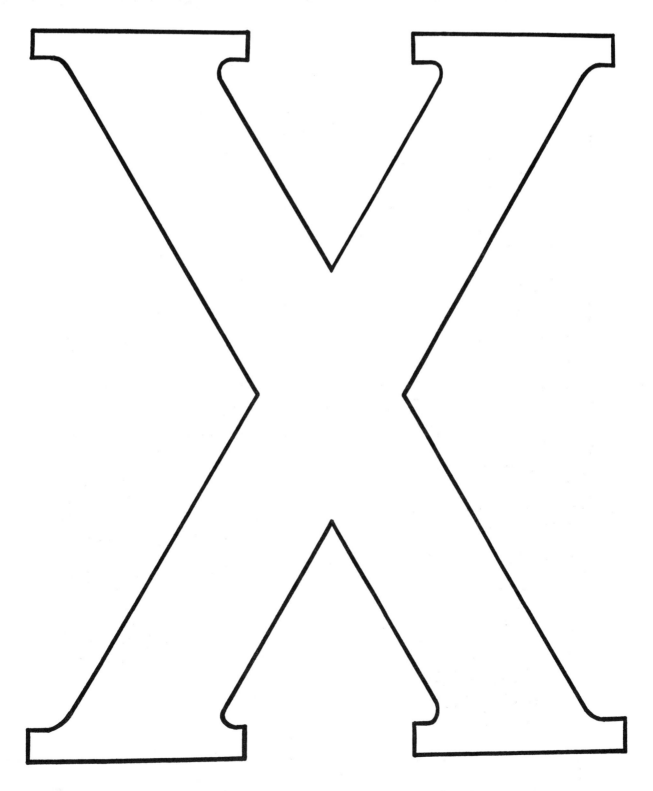

Name _____

X x Puzzle

To solve this puzzle, color the capital **X**'s any color you wish and color the lower case **x**'s silver. What **x** picture did you find?

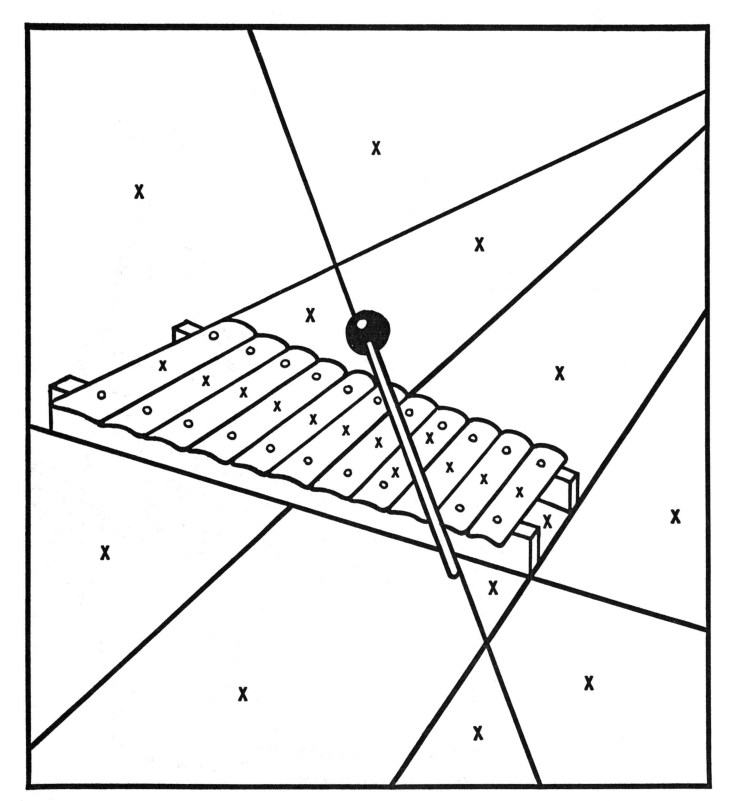

Name _____

X-Caliber's X Biscuits
(Serves 4–6)

You need:

1¾ cups whole-wheat flour
1 teaspoon salt
2½ teaspoons double-acting baking powder
4 tablespoons chilled butter
⅔ to ¾ cups milk

Directions:
Sift the flour, salt, and baking powder into a bowl.
Cut the butter into the dry ingredients using a pastry blender or by slicing through the mixture with a table knife in each hand. Add only enough milk to make the dough workable. Knead the dough on a floured breadboard for several minutes. Roll the dough into 3-inch long strips and make X's on an ungreased baking sheet. Leave room between the X's for the dough to expand when it bakes. Bake the biscuits in a 450° oven for 10 to 13 minutes until golden brown.

Name _____

V W X Letter Review

Practice writing these letters on the lines below. You have mastered the letters V, v, W, w, X, x. Congratulations!

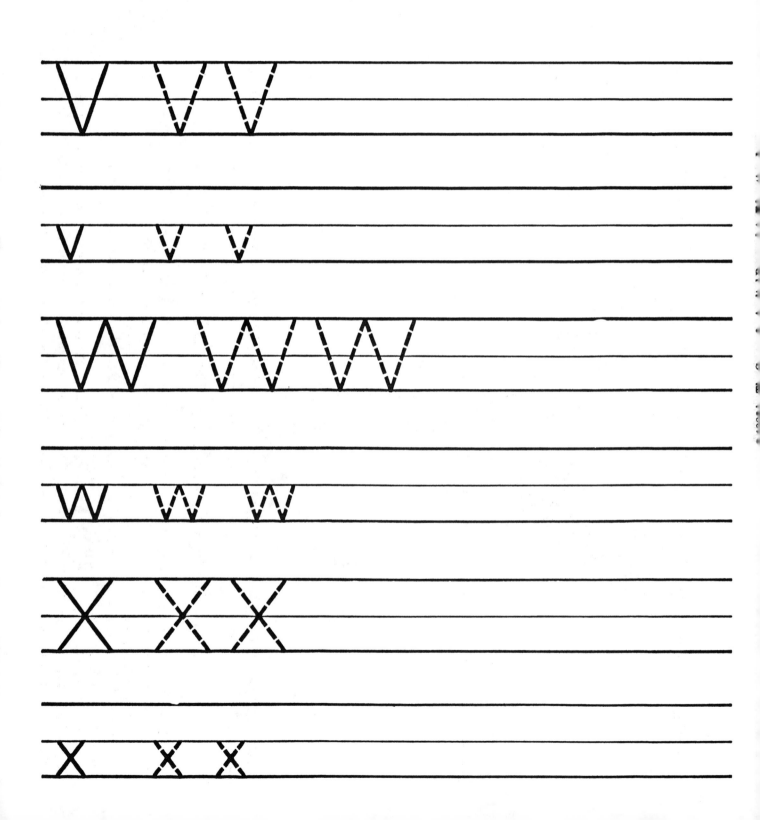

Finger Tracing the Letters Y y

Reproduce this page for each child in your class. Have each child cut along the dotted line and discard the teacher directions. Then help each one glue colored yarn on the heavy black lines using white glue and making sure not to cover up the direction arrows.

When the glue is dry, have each child trace over the letters using the first finger and following the directions indicated by the numbered arrows.

Place the finished letter sheet with the child's name on the back in a shoebox for each child and locate the boxes in a convenient place where the children can practice tracing the letters daily. This will help them remember the names of the letters and the correct way to form them.

Name _____

Yolanda Yak

Yolanda the young yak likes to practice yodeling in the mountains of Yosemite. However, she doesn't realize that it makes many of her animal friends yelp! Draw some things into this picture to solve their problem, then color the page.

ANSWERS: Draw earmuffs on each animal, put Yolanda in a box, etc.

Name _____

Help Yolanda's Young Friend

Yolanda the Yak has a young friend who lives near Yosemite. He does something very important during the week. Help him tell the story of his life. Find the two pictures below the dotted line that tell the end of the story. Cut out these pictures and glue them into the empty spaces.

- -

Name _____

Yolanda's Rhyming Game

Yolanda likes to play rhyming games when she's not yodeling. Here's one of her games that you can play. Here's what you do:

1. Look at the picture in upper left-hand square with its name printed below it.
2. Find all of the pictures in that block that rhyme with this word.
3. Color each of the rhyming words. Good luck!

Name _____

Find Yuri's Differences

Yolanda's good friend Yuri Bear loves to play with toys. Look carefully at these two pictures of Yuri. Circle each place on picture 2 that is different from picture 1. Color the pictures if you like. (Hint: There are 9 things that are different.)

Name _____

Y y Puzzle

To solve this puzzle, color the lower-case y spaces any color you would like. What **y** picture did you find?

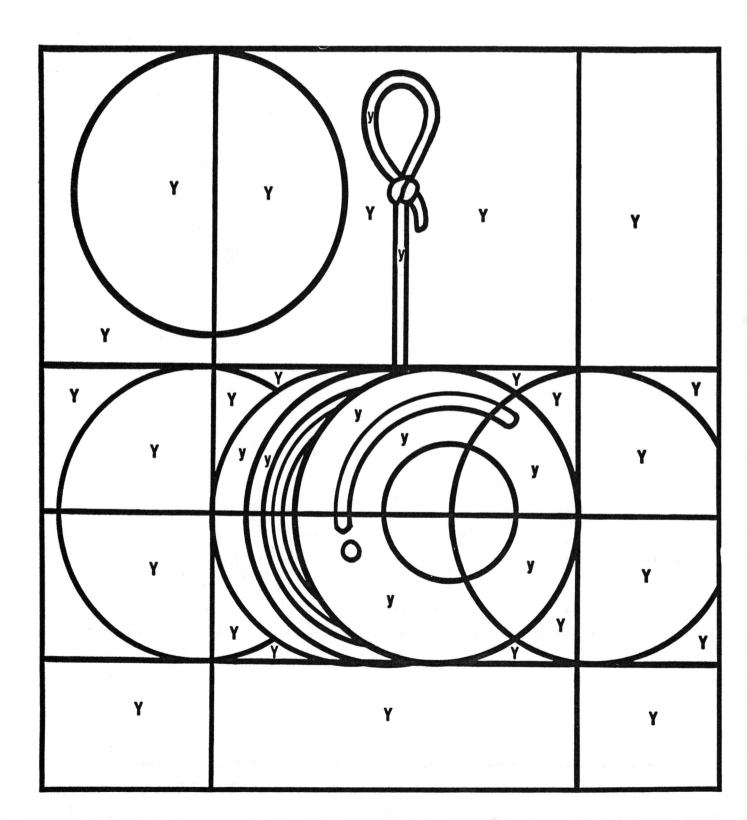

Name _____

Yolanda's Yummy Yams

You need:

1 teaspoon butter
1 29-ounce can yams
1 8-ounce can crushed pineapple
12 large marshmallows

Directions:
Open and drain the can of yams. Butter the bottom and sides of a 2- to 3-quart casserole dish. Place the yams in the buttered casserole. Open the can of drained crushed pineapple and add it to the yams. Then smooth it into an even layer. Place 12 marshmallows on top of the yam mixture. Bake uncovered in a 350° oven for 25 minutes or until the marshmallows are golden brown.

Finger Tracing the Letters Z z

Reproduce this page for each child in your class. Have each child cut along the dotted line and discard the teacher directions. Then help each one glue zigzag rickrack on the heavy black lines using white glue and making sure not to cover up the direction arrows.

When the glue is dry, have each child trace over the letters using the first finger and following the directions indicated by the numbered arrows.

Place the finished letter sheet with the child's name on the back in a shoebox for each child and locate the boxes in a convenient place where the children can practice tracing the letters daily. This will help them remember the names of the letters and the correct way to form them.

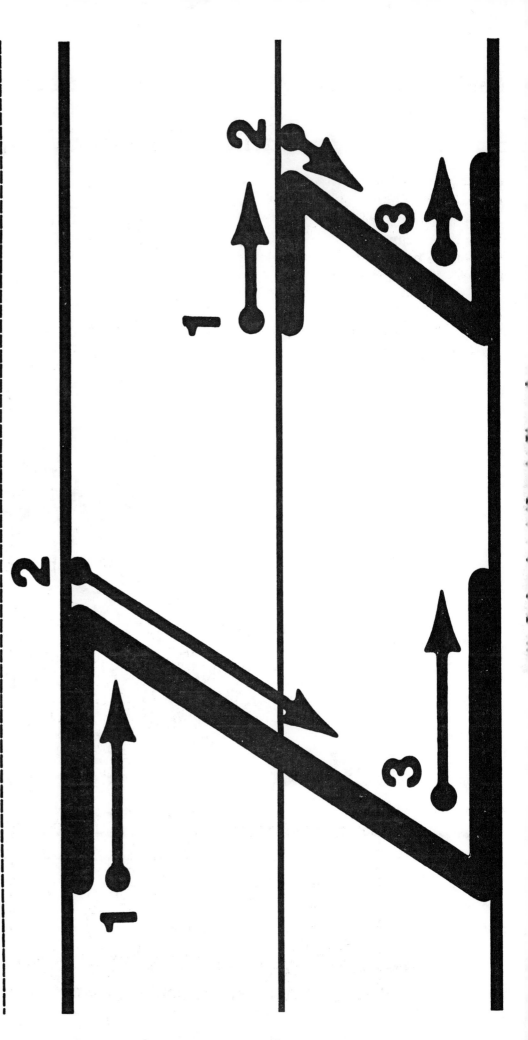

Name _____

Zachary Zebra

Zachary Zebra from Zanzibar was sent to the Zurich Zoo last year. He loved to eat zucchini and zinnias, but the zookeeper, Mr. Zindelbottom, wouldn't let him have any because they made his stripes turn different colors! One day Zachary ate his favorite foods. Color him with all the bright colors that you have.

ZEBRA

Name _____

Zachary's Z Game

Zachary was so angry about not getting his zucchini and zinnias to eat that he ran away from the zoo one night with his friends Zippy, Zelda, and Zana. However, they soon realized that they wouldn't solve their problems by running away, so Zachary and his friends turned back. Help them get back to the zoo by playing the Z game. Here's what you do:

1. Cut out the markers on this page. Cut a slit at the end of each marker on the line, then interlock the slits so that the marker stands up.
2. To play the game, use the gameboard on page Zz-3 and have each player place a marker on the capital **Z.**
3. The player with the most zigzags on his clothing goes first. She tosses a penny in the air. If it lands face up, she moves ahead 2 spaces. If it lands face down, she moves ahead 1 space. The player must name the **z** picture in the space he lands on or follow the directions in the space.
4. The next player wearing the most zigzags goes second in the same way, and the rest of the players do the same. The first player to reach the lower-case **z** is the winner.

Name _____

Name _____

Help Zachary's Friends

Zachary the Zebra has many friends all over the country. Some of his friends live in the forest. In this picture they are looking at something very carefully. Cut out the picture at the bottom of this page that best shows what Zachary's friends could really be looking at. Then color the picture.

Name _____

Z z Puzzle

To solve this puzzle, color all the capital **Z** spaces any color you would like. What **z** picture did you find?

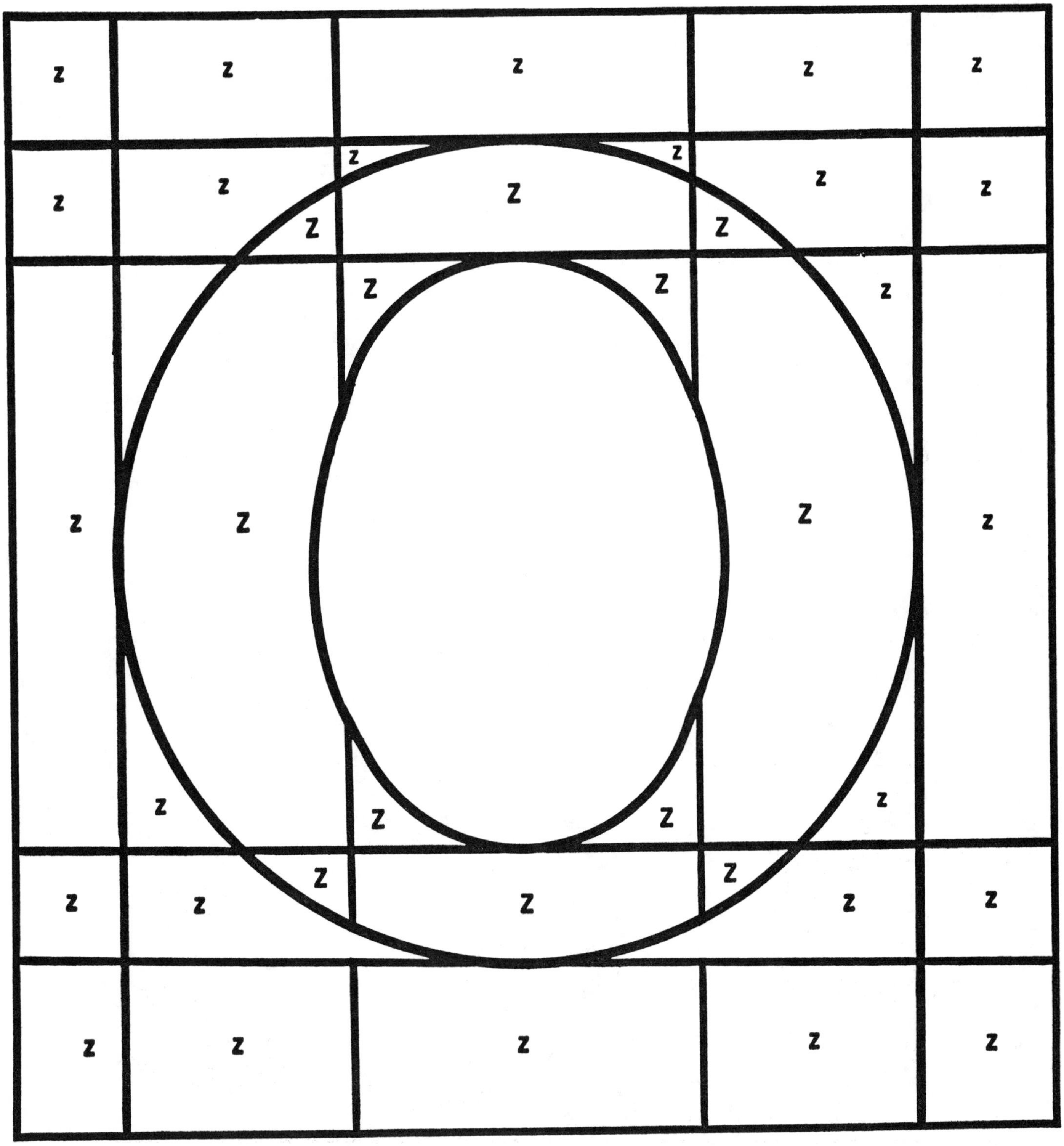

z   z   Z   z   z

z   z   Z   Z   z   z
              Z   Z

                    Z   Z   Z

z   Z   Z   z

     Z   Z   Z   z

     z   Z   Z   Z   z   z

z   z   Z   z   z

Name _____

Zachary's Zoo Sandwiches (Serves 1)

You need:

3 slices of your favorite bread
a sandwich filling (such as tuna,
   egg salad, peanut butter and jelly,
   cream cheese)
decorative tidbits (such as olives,
   pimientos, raisins, nuts)

Directions:
To make one zoo sandwich, cut each piece of bread into the same animal shape. You can use a cookie cutter or cut out and trace one of the animal shapes on this page. Spread your favorite filling on one shape. Place a matching bread shape on top. Spread on more filling and place the third shape on top. Decorate the face and the body with the tidbits. To make standup animals for a zoo parade, use sticky fillings such as peanut butter or cream cheese.

Name _____

Y Z Letter Review

Practice writing these letters on the lines below. You have mastered the letters Y, y, Z, z. Congratulations!

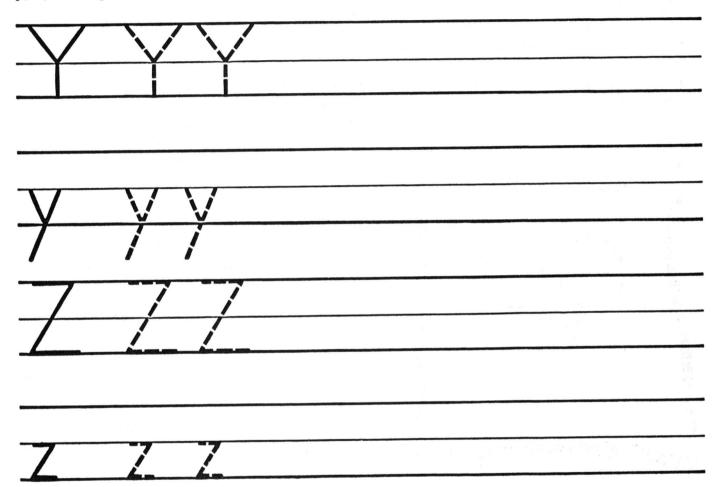